D0859166

Spiritual Transformations

For Elizabeth

With lasting friendship!

Karl

FACETS

Selected Titles in the Facets Series

The Stem Cell Debate
Ted Peters

Technology and Human Becoming
Philip Hefner

Darwin and Intelligent Design
Francisco J. Ayala

Virtues and Values
Peter J. Paris

Christian Faith and Religious Diversity
John B. Cobb Jr.

Divine Justice, Divine Judgment
Dan O. Via

Real Peace, Real Security
Sharon D. Welch

Spiritual Transformations

Science, Religion, and Human Becoming

Karl E. Peters

Fortress Press
Minneapolis

SPIRITUAL TRANSFORMATIONS
Science, Religion, and Human Becoming

Cover photo © Imagewerks RF / Getty Images.
Cover and book design: Joseph Bonyata

Library of Congress Cataloging-in-Publication Data
Peters, Karl Edward, 1939–
    Spiritual transformations : science, religion, and human becoming /
Karl E. Peters.
        p. cm.
    Includes bibliographical references.
    ISBN-13: 978-0-8006-6320-9 (alk. paper)
1. Experience (Religion) 2. Conversion. 3. Psychology, Religious.
I. Title.
BL53.P395 2008
204'.2–dc22   2008007894

12   11   10   09   08   1   2   3   4   5   6   7   8   9   10

Contents

Preface
vii

1. On the Edge of Time
1

2. Crossings
15

3. Passages
27

4. Rebirths
39

5. Conversion
51

6. Callings
70

7. Events of Grace
82

8. Calamitous Convergences
96

9. Dying
109

10. Living Now in Eternity
122

Notes
139

Preface

This book is about the variety of spiritual transformations we can experience. It is about those transformative experiences that shape and reshape who we are and our relationships with other human beings, the rest of our world, and the sacred. It is about experiences of human becoming that help us live more effective lives for our own well-being, the well-being of other human beings, and the well-being of all creatures on our planetary home, Earth.

For all of my professional life—the past forty years—I've tried to do my religious thinking in relation to experience. I've tried to reflect about religion in relation to my own life experience, the life experiences reported by others, and the experiences that are the basis of the ideas of contemporary science. Another way of saying this is that I have tried to be empirical in my theology.

Empirical theology—we might say experiential theology—is to be found in the Bible, for example, in the Hebrew prophets who tried to understand the meaning of historical events as the activity of God. Experiential theology is also a basis of the thinking of early Christians as they tried to comprehend the meaning of their experience of Jesus. Experience is prominent in Buddhism—in Siddhartha Gautama's enlightenment about the alleviation of suffering. And experience has been the basis of much of American religion and religious thought—from the Christian emphasis on experiencing Jesus as one's Lord and Savior in revival movements to the more formal discipline known as American empirical theology.

In American empirical theology one finds two different but related movements. One grows out of what can be called *classical empiricism* and the other is expressed as *radical empiricism*. Classical empiricism focuses on discrete sense perceptions as a way to experience the world and to test ideas about what is experienced. An important part of the scientific method is the appeal to this kind of experience. Radical empiricism holds that experience includes not only sense perceptions but also feelings in relation to what is experienced. Following William James, it also holds that our initial experience of something is an experience of a whole, and this includes the experience of the person in relation to the whole. It is thinking that analyzes the whole experience into discrete sense impressions, particular feelings, and their relationships.[1]

The distinction between classical and radical empiricism had led to two types of empirical theology in American religious thought. Philosopher of religion Nancy Frankenberry sums up the difference as follows: "Some empirical theologians restrict the term 'knowledge' to that which involves interpretation, reflection, and prediction." "Prediction" refers to what can be observed. Others "prefer to widen the term 'knowledge' so as to include the mode of acquaintance by which what is directly given is grasped feelingly, and feeling is taken to have cognitive import."[2]

How does all this talk about different kinds of experiences inform this book? First, spiritual transformation is a particular kind of experience. As we move through the book we will look at a variety of experiences of spiritual transformation, which I have labeled with metaphors such as "crossings" (chapter 2), "passages" (chapter 3), "rebirths" (chapter 4), "conversion" (chapter 5), "callings" (chapter 6), "events of grace" (chapter 7), "calamitous convergences" (chapter 8), and "dying" (chapter 9). Metaphors not only describe these experiences. They also help us to highlight their significance for our lives. Some of these experiences will be my own. In fact, some chapters can be understood as parts of my own spiritual autobiography. Other experiences of spiritual transformation will be those reported by others. It is my hope that the concrete examples in these pages will lead you to recall some experiences of spiritual transformation in your own life.

Second, scientifically grounded experience—the type of experience I've identified as classical empiricism—underlies my presentation of the natural world as a series of transformations in the evolutionary history of the universe. While I will give references to work based on this kind of experience, I will not go into detail about the scientific method and its particular results. This method, often with the aid of technology, such as telescopes and microscopes, has helped create a plausible story of the fourteen-billion-year history of the universe, which I briefly outline in chapter 1.

When, as an empirical theologian, I adhere to the clearly defined and carefully analyzed experience of science (classical empiricism), I see this evolutionary history in terms of a sacred, nonpersonal process of creative transformation. However, when I pay attention to what I feel in particular experiences of spiritual transformation (radical empiricism), I am led to think that I may be in touch with and guided by some kind of personal presence. I'm also led to suggest that the science-based evolutionary history of the universe may also be shaped by a personal divine presence. The classical and radical empirical ways of knowing how transformations occur is part of the contrast between the way contemporary science looks at things and the way traditional cultures look at our experiences of the world.

One theme that runs through many chapters is that spiritual transformation is death and rebirth. Because we live in a world that is constantly changing, we cannot help but experience the loss of things as they pass away. However, it is precisely this passing away that allows new things to be born and that allows for growth and development—for human becoming.

When most of us experience spiritual transformation, we experience it as individuals. In this book, I suggest that spiritual transformation is experienced not just as any kind of change, but as the kind of change that has three facets. One facet is a change that brings us into our sacred center—God within. Another is an experience of transformative change from fragmentation to well-functioning wholeness. A third facet is a shift from self-preoccupation toward loving others and all creation. Spiritual transformation in all these aspects helps us live more effectively for ourselves, other humans, and the rest of the planet.

In looking at these facets, I'll be looking primarily at the transformation of individuals. However, in chapter 2, I'll also suggest that what the Hebrews experienced in the Exodus from Egypt is a societal spiritual transformation. And, in various places in the book, I will imply that our own individual transformations need to become worldwide. This implication becomes explicit in chapter 11, "Living Now in Eternity," where I suggest that each of us is being called to live in ways that benefit not only us but everything that is in a process of becoming on planet Earth.

The opportunity for developing these ideas occurred in 2005, when I gave a series of six chapel

talks at the annual conference of the Institute on
Religion in an Age of Science (IRAS). The conference
theme was "Varieties of Spiritual Transformation:
Scientific and Religious Perspectives," and it was
organized and chaired by Andrew B. Newberg and
me. The conference took place at the Star Island
Conference Center, ten miles off the coast from
Portsmouth, New Hampshire.[3] I am grateful to
those at the conference who urged me to make my
talks public.

I also want to thank Kevin Sharpe, editor of the
Theology and Science series at Fortress Press, for
suggesting that my manuscript might be a book in
the Facets series. The suggestions of Michael West,
Editor-in-Chief at Fortress, have been very helpful
in the further development of this work. So have
the support and questions of members of an adult
education class at my church. I appreciate Alice
Evans and Marye Gail Harrison for their excellent
clarifying suggestions. Finally, I want to thank
Marjorie H. Davis, my wife and companion of
mind and heart. Her stimulating suggestions and
careful editorial work through many drafts have
greatly improved the readability of this book.

As I've further developed, expanded, rear-
ranged, and added new chapters to my Star Island
talks, I've enjoyed remembering many experiences
at this special place. It was at IRAS conferences
on Star Island that I became acquainted early in
my career with the vast history of our evolving
universe and with the religious significance of this

history. It also was on Star Island that I had one of the most memorable religious experiences of my life, described near the end of chapter 4. As you read about some of my Star Island memories, I invite you to think about how special places and times in your own lives have contributed to your own meaningful spiritual experiences. Now I invite you to continue your thinking with me as we begin to reflect on what it means to be spiritually transformed "On the Edge of Time."

1

On the Edge of Time

Reading: The "Cry"

Nikos Kazantzakis in *Report to Greco* describes the process of evolution as the result of a divine creative activity. He personifies this activity as a "Cry."[1]

> Blowing through heaven and earth, and in our hearts and the heart of every living thing, is a gigantic breath—a great Cry—which we call God. Plant life wished to continue its motionless sleep next to stagnant waters, but the Cry leaped up within it and violently shook its roots: "Away, let go of the earth, walk!" Had the tree been able to think and judge, it would have cried, "I don't want to. What are you urging me to do? You are demanding the impossible!" But the Cry, without pity, kept shaking its roots and shouting, "Away, let go of the earth, walk!"
>
> It shouted in this way for thousands of eons; and lo! as a result of desire and struggle, life escaped the motionless tree and was liberated.

Animals appear—worms—making themselves at home in water and mud. "We're just fine here," they said. "We have peace and security; we're not budging!"

But the terrible Cry hammered itself pitilessly into their loins. "Leave the mud, stand up, give birth to your betters!"

"We don't want to! We can't!"

"You can't, but I can. Stand up!"

And lo! After thousands of eons, humans emerged, trembling on their still unsolid legs.

The human being is a centaur; our equine hoofs are planted in the ground, but our body from breast to head is worked on and tormented by the merciless Cry. We have been fighting, again for thousands of eons, to draw ourselves, like a sword, out of our animalistic scabbard. We are also fighting—and this is our new struggle— to draw ourselves out of our human scabbard. Humanity calls in despair, "Where can I go? I have reached the pinnacle, beyond is the abyss." And the Cry answers, "I am beyond. Stand up!" All things are centaurs. If this were not the case, the world would rot into inertness and sterility.

Reflection: On the Edge of Time

Several years ago, I was driving down a street in Winter Park, Florida, on my way to a class at Rollins College. Winter Park has these lovely southern oak trees that create canopies over the streets. The sun was behind me, streaming down through the trees and giving everything a warm, early morning glow. As I drove, I was reflecting on a course I was teaching, a science and religion course on evolution and creation. I was thinking about the fourteen-billion-year history of the universe.

Suddenly I realized that I was on the edge, the edge of the universe. This was not the edge of space but the edge of time. I realized that the whole universe had taken fourteen billion years to bring me, and everything else, to the moment I was in. All that time, all that creative activity bringing into being galaxies, stars, our planet Earth, life, and me. Wow! I was awestruck. I still am.

We all are on the edge of time—right now, in every moment. Each of us is a special form of energy-matter that has been created through a series of transformations over fourteen billion years. And on our edge of time, we are always going into the future. It is an unknown future. Yet it is a future upon which our thinking and actions will make a difference. We help create the future. Our thoughts and actions shape what the future will be like. What a responsibility! What kind of future are we being called to create? I'll consider these questions in chapter 10.

In this chapter, I'd like to reflect with you on what it means to live on the edge of time in a universe that continually undergoes a variety of transformations. I'll sketch some of the transformations in the history of the universe that have brought us to this point. This will set a wider context of meaning for understanding some facets of human spiritual transformation in our human becoming.

One way to narrate the history of the universe is as a series of transformations that bring new phases of the universe into being. The basic stuff of the universe is energy-matter. In keeping with the first law of thermodynamics, energy-matter is neither created nor destroyed. However, as the universe expanded and cooled down after the big bang, energy began to be transformed into matter, into subatomic particles and simple atoms—hydrogen, helium, and a very small amount of lithium. These atoms formed huge clouds that become galaxies and the first stars.

A second transformation occurred when some early massive stars—stars ten times the mass of our sun—burned up all their hydrogen fuel in nuclear fusion. They then went through a process of dying, ending in a tremendous explosion called a supernova. In the extreme temperatures of supernovae, elements more complex than hydrogen and helium were created—oxygen, nitrogen, carbon, phosphorus, iron, and so on. Out of these elements and more interstellar hydrogen and helium, new stars were created. Some of these had planets. Our sun and its planets, including Earth, were formed about five billion years ago out of the debris of earlier, exploded stars.

On Earth, further transformations took place as atoms formed molecules and as some molecules became more complex and self-replicating. Life came into being. Once life occurred, about 3.5 to 4 billion years ago, Darwinian evolution took over, creating millions of forms of life. One aspect of evolving life is the nervous system. Through Darwinian evolution, simple nervous systems, such as those found in worms, evolved into more complex nervous systems, until there came into being nervous systems that were complex enough to think with symbols—human brains. Our brains are capable of creating complex languages and mathematical formulae—making us what anthropologist Terry Deacon calls the "symbolic species"[2] or making us what theologian Gordon Kaufman calls "bio-historical" beings, beings shaped by both biology and the symbols and practices of human history.[3]

More transformations occurred in human society and culture. Human beings originally evolved with biological tendencies that helped motivate us to care for genetically close kin and to engage in small-group, reciprocal altruism. With the invention of morality, economics, politics, and religions, these small-scale communities were transformed into larger, cooperating societies and multi-national civilizations. A question for the future is whether these large-scale societies and civilizations can evolve into a peaceful, cooperating worldwide community, living in harmony with the rest of the earth. Or will evolution's "human experiment" end in a nuclear holocaust or in environmental disaster?

What all these transformations mean is that each of us is made up of the energy present fourteen billion years ago at the origin of our universe. We also are made up of atoms of oxygen, nitrogen, carbon, phosphorus, and iron created in the explosive deaths of massive stars. Likewise, we are the descendants of a one-celled organism that was the first replicating life on our planet almost four billion years ago. More particularly, we have evolved from a tiny mouse-like creature that was present at the time of the dinosaurs. When an asteroid collided with the earth sixty-six million years ago, causing the extinction of the dinosaurs, this mouse-like creature (like a tree shrew) began to flourish, leading to the common ancestor of chimpanzees, bonobos, and human beings. Finally, in this evolutionary history, we are the inheritors of many of the inventions, values, and thoughts of countless human beings that have gone before us on planet Earth. Each of us stands in our own unique way on the edge of time—able to continue in our own small way the legacy of energy, atoms, molecules, life, and culture that has evolved to give us the gift of our own existence.

A couple of years ago I found myself on the edge of time on Star Island, attending the 2005 conference of the Institute on Religion in an Age of Science. As I mentioned in the preface, the conference theme was "Varieties of Spiritual Transformation: Scientific and Religious Perspectives." The goal of the conference was to understand better the relation between new knowledge about spiritual transformation from the sciences, especially neuroscience and the social sciences, and the experientially based wisdom of religious traditions. As the chapel speaker at this conference, my goal was to encourage people to reflect on some of the varieties of spiritual transformation and their outcomes, while drawing on my knowledge of world religions and evolutionary science.

I also hoped to learn from other speakers and participants. As I listened to various speakers talk about spiritual transformation, I was asking myself the question, "What is meant by the term *spiritual transformation*?" One way of thinking I wanted to avoid was that the spiritual is something opposed to material—the kind of dualistic thinking that in the past has so often separated the core of the human person (the soul) from our bodies. Because the work of many scientists has led me to believe that one cannot separate our inner, subjective states from the workings of our brain and body, I did not want to think of spiritual transformation as involving something independent of our embodied life. I also did not want to think that spiritual transformation is something so unusual that only a few people, for example the great mystics, could have spiritual transformations. Because of my belief that the sacred is present in all aspects of the world and of human life, I was looking for ways in which spiritual transformations could be everyday kinds of events.

As I listened to the other speakers, I began to realize two things. First, for some it seemed that a spiritual transformation is a change in identity—a change in who we are in terms of our conceptions of ourselves and our relationships with others and the wider world. Second, it seemed that transformations begin to occur when our lives are challenged and disrupted in such a way that we can no longer think of ourselves in the same way, have the same relationships, or participate in the same basic rhythms of our lives. We are continuously becoming.

We might think of our identities as involving three "dimensions."[4] The first draws on the idea that we are individual, embodied selves. As I said above, I do not wish to distinguish who we are from the states of our bodies and brains. This means that our identities are closely related to our subjective experiences of ourselves and also our experiences of the world around us. Our identities are also related to how we express ourselves and act in the world. So, when something in our body changes, for example during puberty when hormones and body appearances change, our identities also change. When this happens, many cultures have rites of passage that initiate their children into adulthood.

Likewise, as our bodies age, we also undergo a change in who we are. Our inner experiences of ourselves change when we develop the aches and pains of arthritis, for example. Our experiences of the world change as we, for example, develop cataracts, macular degeneration, or hearing loss. And how we act in the world changes as our physical abilities become more limited. All this means that our identities also change: we become "old folks." However, we have accumulated a lifetime of experience, and so, in some societies this means we become identified and respected as wise elders.

A second dimension of our identity is in our relationships with others. As we go though life, we become different people as we assume different roles in relation to others: child, teenager, married person, parent, school teacher, skilled mechanic, computer operator, priest, and so on. Each of these involves us in different sets of relationships with others, as well as different ways in which we experience ourselves and understand the meaning and significance of our lives. As our relationships change, we undergo a second facet of spiritual transformation in terms of who we are.

The third dimension involves our relation to the sacred, that which is most important or significant in our lives, which many call God. It is that with which we are "ultimately concerned" according to theologian Paul Tillich.[5] Henry Nelson Wieman suggests it is that which elicits our "ultimate commitment."[6] William May speaks of it as involving the fundamental rhythms of our lives.[7] Our fundamental rhythms include the way we get up and go to bed, the way we dress, the various routine events of our day as we go through a week, month and year. I remember experiencing these rhythms as a young child with my mother. On Mondays she would do the laundry, on Tuesdays the ironing, on Wednesdays volunteer work, and so on, until she worshiped on Sundays. For me, this pattern was a part of who she was. Whole societies live according to weekly rhythms culminating in a Sabbath, monthly rhythms following the lunar cycle, annual rhythms of planting and harvest, or rhythms related to the equinoxes in our Earth-Sun system. Some of these annual rhythms are linked to historical events such as Christian Advent and Easter, or Jewish Passover. Many of these rhythms are manifest in religious rituals. When these rhythms change, people's identities change. Even the identity of a society can change.

What causes these rhythms to change? What changes the ways we experience and act towards ourselves and the world? What changes the ways we relate to others? In many cases, as I've suggested above, it is the natural course of our lives, in which biology and society play a role. In other times, it can be a positive set of special circumstances that leads to a new friendship, a new school community, a job promotion, or the birth of a grandchild. At other times identity transformation occurs in negative circumstances, such as when one suffers a serious disease, or the death of a friend, spouse, sibling, parent, or child. Transformations may be triggered by natural and human caused disasters—Hurricane Katrina, the Indonesian tsunami of 2004, 9/11, or any number of wars in the twentieth and twenty-first centuries. All these—a variety of individual, social, and natural events—can contribute to transformations of self-understanding and identity, changes in our relationships with others, and shifts in the basic rhythms of our lives.

All that I've described and more may be included in a scientifically grounded working definition of *spiritual transformation.* The Spiritual Transformation Scientific Research Program headed by anthropologist Solomon Katz suggests that spiritual transformations are "dramatic changes in world and self views, purposes, religious beliefs, attitudes, and behavior."[8] If one adds the idea of the transcendent or the sacred, we can also consider psychologist Ken Pargament's suggestion that "spiritual transformation refers primarily to a fundamental change in the place of the sacred or the character of the sacred as an object of significance in the life of the individual, and secondarily to a fundamental change in the pathways the individual takes to the sacred."[9]

Humanity's religions exhibit many different ways of thinking about the sacred. Sometimes it is thought of as many personal spiritual beings that underlie the workings of nature and human life. Sometimes the sacred is thought of as one supreme reality—the God of Western monotheism. Sometimes it is thought of in nonpersonal terms as the way of Heaven and Earth, or the Tao, in Chinese thought. The sacred can also be identified as the creativity in nature and human history.

In all these understandings, however, two things seem to be present. Whether it is thought of as many or one, personal or nonpersonal, the sacred is, first, the source of all existence and, second, that in relation to which our lives become meaningful. It is understood as something more than ourselves in which we "live and move and have our being."[10] It is that which, in various ways, calls us and the world, on the edge of time, to move beyond present states of existence. It is like the "Cry" that Kazantzakis poetically portrays in the reading at the beginning of this chapter.

One way to understand the sacred is by distinguishing between creator and created. This is an important distinction in Judaism, Christianity, and Islam. In some of the major expressions of these religions, all of God's creation is good, and God, as the creator, the source of the world, is the greatest good. Genesis 1 affirms this when, after each phase of creation, God looks at what has been created and sees that it is good. Augustine, a Christian theologian in the fourth and fifth centuries c.e., develops this idea in contrast to a powerful form of dualism present in his day, Manichaeism. Manichaeism held that the world is a battleground between two opposing ultimate forces, one good and one evil. Instead, Augustine followed the thinking of the Neoplatonists, the followers of the Greek philosopher Plato. He reasoned that all existence is good, that evil is only a negative concept, and that the source of all existence, God, is the highest good. So humans should not become addicted to the goods of this world, should not be in bondage to such goods. This has been called idolatry. Instead they are called to turn toward a relationship with the highest good—God.[11]

This distinction between all of creation as good and the creator being the greatest good is also advanced by the twentieth-century philosopher of religion Henry Nelson Wieman. In *The Source of Human Good*, Wieman does not think of God as a being beyond the world who creates the world but, instead, as the process of creative transformation within the world. Everything in the world is good. It can be good in itself or good because it is instrumental to something else that is good. It also can be both intrinsically and instrumentally good. Wieman uses the idea of "relations of mutual support" as a way of generally characterizing what is good. When things are in mutually supporting relationships, they are good. One example is health, a state in which all parts of an organism work well together as a whole. Another example is meaning, a system of mutually supportive ideas and experiences in terms of which a human being can see his or her place in the larger scheme of things. Love also is such a good, the mutually supporting relationships of feelings and behaviors between two people. Families and communities of all kinds are other examples; whenever their members live and work together in supportive ways, good is present.

Still greater than any of these kinds of relations of mutual support is that which creates health, meaning, love, and community. Wieman calls this "creative good," and also "creative process," "creative interchange," and "creative transformation." Because it is the source of all intrinsic and instrumental good, Wieman calls this process *God*.[12]

So, as a first attempt at understanding what *spiritual transformation* means, we might say that spiritual transformations are those transformations that occur when we are caught up in the creative process that continually transforms the world to produce new relationships of mutual support—new systems of existence, life, and human society. For individual humans, such transformations bring about new forms of human self-understanding, human relationships, and new relationships with the wider world—new forms of identity. Such transformations can be regarded as "God-working" continuously and creatively on the edge of time throughout the history of the universe. The more we are involved in spiritual transformations—growing in self-understanding and in relationships with others—we participate in that process. Thus our relationship to God also grows as we live more and more of our lives in relationship with the sacred. In the chapters that follow, I shall explore some of the ways in which we can undergo changes in identity and in our relationship with the sacred during our life journeys on the edge of time.

2

Crossings

Reading: The Buddhist Ferryboat

In his book, *Philosophies of India*, Heinrich Zimmer writes the following about the Buddhist ferryboat, the vehicle to enlightenment:[1]

Among the conversations of the Buddha . . . there appears a discourse on the value of the vehicle of the doctrine. First, the Buddha describes a person who, like himself or any of his followers, becomes filled with a loathing of the perils and delights of secular existence. That person decides to quit the world and cross the stream of life to the far land of spiritual safety. Collecting wood and reeds, she or he builds a raft, and by this means succeeds in attaining the other shore. The Buddha confronts his monks, then, with the question.

"What would be your opinion of this person— would he be a clever person, if, out of gratitude for the raft and . . . having reached the other shore, he should cling to it, take it on his back, and walk about with the weight of it?" [The disciples agree with the Buddha that the proper attitude toward the raft is that it is a tool to be used but then discarded once the other shore is reached.]

The Buddha then concludes, "In the same way the vehicle of doctrine is to be cast away and forsaken, once the other shore of Enlightenment (*nirvana*) has been attained."

[What then does happen when one reaches the other shore?] Not only the raft, but the stream too, becomes void of reality for the one who has attained the other shore. When such a one turns to look again at the land left behind, what does she see? What *can* one see who has crossed the horizon beyond which there is no duality? One looks—and there *is* no "other shore"; there is no torrential separating river; there is no raft; there is no ferryman; there can have been no crossing of the nonexistent stream. The whole scene of the two banks and the river between is simply gone. There can be no such thing for the enlightened eye and mind, because to see or think of anything as something "other" . . . would mean that full Enlightenment had not yet been attained. . . . Illumination means that the delusory distinction between the two shores of a worldly and a transcendental existence no longer holds. There *is* no stream of rebirths flowing between two separated shores: no *samsara* and no *nirvana*.

Moreover, there is no Buddhism—no boat, since there are neither shores nor waters between. There is no boat, and there is no boatman—no Buddha.

Reflection: Crossings

For over three decades—almost every year—I have made a crossing. A ten mile crossing from Portsmouth, New Hampshire, on the United States mainland to Star Island to attend the annual conference of the Institute on Religion in an Age of Science (IRAS). During the opening orientation session, I often experience one of the customs on Star Island. Because it is an island in the midst of the Isles of Shoals, all attending the conference are welcomed with the explanation that there are two kinds of Shoalers. People attending for the first time are welcomed as "New Shoalers." Others who have been on the island before are "Old Shoalers." So all are Shoalers, and one can ask, what qualifies one to be a Shoaler? It is the simple fact of crossing the waters of the north Atlantic from Portsmouth to Star Island. This crossing might be regarded as a small transformation, a small change in identity from life on the mainland to becoming Shoalers—members of the Isles of Shoals community for the week of the conference.

I remember well my first crossing to Star Island. It was in 1972, and I'd come up on the bus from New York City. On the bus I met a woman who turned out to be an Old Shoaler. She was a professor of nursing at the City University of New York and had been going to Star Island for several years. I don't remember her name now, but I remember something she said: "Probably the first thing that you'll want to do when you arrive on Star Island is to get right back on the boat and return to the mainland."

Maybe she planted a seed in my mind, because that is exactly what I felt as I arrived and looked at this strange island. In some way all crossings take us to strange lands. To someone who had grown up in the fields and woodlands of Wisconsin, Star Island looked like a barren rock with its huge structure of a wooden hotel on top of it. It was indeed strange to me. But I didn't get back on the boat, and I've been going there ever since.

One of my crossings to Star Island was in 1984 to the conference titled "Recent Discoveries in Neurobiology: Do They Matter for Religion, the Social Sciences, and the Humanities." It was a conference that was organized in light of the thinking of the well-known anthropologist Victor Turner. It was hoped that Turner would be one of the key speakers, but unfortunately he passed away before the conference was held. So, instead of hearing him in person, we celebrated Turner's life and thought.[2]

At that conference, I first heard about Turner's stages of transformation and his concept of "liminality." *Liminality* means "threshold" in Latin. Since that occasion, I've encountered Turner's concepts elsewhere, for example, in a book titled *Religions of Asia*, which I've used in a course. The first chapter by John Fenton outlines a model for comparing world religions.[3] One of the themes of that model is the theme of transformation. In fact,

Fenton makes it clear that transformation is one of the fundamental themes of any religion.

The model is fairly simple. It's something we can all recognize, and it's implied in our reading about the Buddhist ferryboat. First, we find ourselves, for any number of reasons, in a problem state, dissatisfied with the way things are—with the way we are. Sometimes this occurs naturally as we outgrow earlier developmental stages in the course of our life. At other times, it can be forced on us by circumstances beyond our control. Second, we become distanced from our usual routines. We enter strange lands as we search for a new way of living or thinking until, third, we cross a threshold—sometimes very suddenly and dramatically. This threshold crossing is the liminal state. Then fourth, out of that threshold crossing, we are reborn into a new understanding, a new identity, or a new way of living. In that new way we return to daily life—transformed.[4]

The state of liminality is the turning point in a process of transformation. It is part of a crossing, one of many crossings that human beings make. For example, the crossing may be an entry into the sanctuary of a church or into the climax point of a religious ritual. It may be entering into a state of meditation. It may be going on a retreat. It may be going to a special place in nature, sometimes only visualized in our minds. For me, it has also been crossing the waters to Star Island. At the conference, in my chapel talks I raised the question: can a week on Star Island become a liminal place and time? Can it become a threshold to some new self-understandings and new ways of doing things in our lives?

Crossing the waters is a central metaphor for spiritual transformation in Buddhism. One of the two major branches of Buddhism is Mahayana Buddhism. The word *yana* means "ferryboat," and *maha* means "great." Mahayana is the great ferryboat that takes people from one shore to the other. The ferryboat is the Buddha, the teachings of the Buddha or the doctrine, and the Buddhist community—the *sangha*. This shore is called *samsara*. It's the life of rebirth and suffering according to Buddhism. Why is it a life of suffering? First, even though we experience things in our world as impermanent and constantly changing, we still become attached to them. We become attached to people. We become attached to ideas. We become attached to ways of living. However, when we become attached to the way things now are, they still change. For example, friends move away; ideas are challenged by new ideas; and how we live can be altered by natural disasters. Instead of going with the flow we try to hang on to the old ways. This creates internal suffering as we try to cling to things that refuse to stay the same.

Underlying our attachment is something that Buddhism calls ignorance—an ignorance that sets up dualities: I and others, things we fear and things we desire. It is an ignorance that allows us to see ourselves as small egos, which should be preserved as precious. But everything is constantly changing. So as we become attached to ourselves, others, and the things of the world in this dualistic ignorance, when they change and die—when they pass away—we suffer. This is our situation on this shore.

According to one school of Buddhist thought, the non-dualistic school (of which we have an example in our reading by Zimmer), the other shore is a state of nonduality. It is sometimes called *nirvana*—extinguishing the flame of desire. When one reaches this state called the other shore, one discovers that there is no ego and no other—no "I," no "you." There is no Buddha, no teachings of the Buddha, no Buddhist community—no ferryboat. These are all distinctions made in a state of dualistic thinking. And, most surprising, there is no shore from which one has traveled and no other shore that one has reached. So nondual Buddhists say things like, "*Samsara* (the realm of suffering) is *nirvana* (the state of bliss)." You can't even make the distinction between samsara and nirvana. If you do, it's a sign that you are not quite there, not quite in an enlightened state.

Well, what can we make of this strange way of thinking? My own take on it is that, when one has reached the other shore, one is also on this shore of everyday life but has been transformed into a state of having no attachments, no desires. One is neither trying to hang on nor having to let go. Rather, one is in a state of serene calm, free of conflict, accepting all things as they are—as they flow in and out of one's life and mind.

So crossing the waters is, for Buddhism, an inner journey of an individual person—via the Buddha's way of thinking, acting, living, and meditating— to reach a state of nondifferentiating tranquility. It is a state in which one can accept everything as it comes and goes. In accepting all things as they are in the present moment, one acknowledges their immediate worth. And, when one sees how others are caught in the snares of attachment and ignorance, this acceptance of the immediate worth of all leads to compassion—compassion right now for all human beings, compassion right now for all living beings.

A quite different crossing of the waters is found in ancient Judaism. It is the crossing of the Red Sea in the Exodus narrative. In contrast with Buddhism, this crossing is not individual but communal. It's a crossing from a state of slavery and oppression into a state of liberation. It's also a crossing in which a new society is created as people of God. And it is establishing a whole new way of life for that people. It's a way of life that, in the words of Rabbi Louis Finkelstein, "endeavors to transform virtually every human action into a means of communion with God. Through this communion with God, the Jew is enabled to make his or her contribution to the establishment of the Kingdom of God and the brotherhood of human beings on earth."[5]

Finkelstein continues that Judaism does this, as far as its adherents are concerned, by seeking "to extend the concept of right and wrong to every aspect of their behavior. Jewish rules of conduct apply not merely to worship, ceremonial, and justice" among humans, "but also to such matters as philosophy, personal friendships and kindnesses, intellectual pursuits, artistic creation, courtesy, and preservation of health, and the care of diet."[6] All of this is to help bring about a transformation—not just a transformation of individuals but a transformation of society, even a transformation of the earth itself. The reason for the crossing of the Red Sea is both the liberation of a people from slavery and a call for them to make the earth and human society a holy place.

So crossing the waters can be a metaphor both for individual spiritual transformation as in Buddhism and for societal transformation in the formation of a people and in making our world holy. I would consider both of these to be major kinds of transformation—we might say extraordinary transformations. Catherine Albanese, a historian of religion, in her book *America: Religions and Religion*, talks about extraordinary and ordinary religion.[7] All of religion is *religion*, but extraordinary religion is the kind of thing we've been talking about, thus far.

Ordinary religion is the kind of religion that goes on in one's daily life and in weekly worship services. This leads me to ask, must spiritual transformations always be extraordinary? Can some be more everyday, more ordinary? Can, for example, crossing the waters of the north Atlantic to a religion and science conference be part of someone's life journey that leads to an ordinary, small-scale spiritual transformation? Let me respond to these questions by offering for your reflection the following incident that was told to me by Marjorie Davis.[8]

In 1977, Marj came to her first Star Island conference of the IRAS. She is now a past president of IRAS, but in 1977 she became acquainted with George Riggan, who was a leader and past president of IRAS. George was a professor of theology at Hartford Seminary, and Marj had heard a series of lectures on science and religion that George had given in the Hartford, Connecticut, area.

Marj says that she resonated with George's thinking. She had a master's degree in neurology and had taught high school biology, chemistry, and physics. She also had always been active in her church. When she asked George how she could learn more about the science and religion he spoke of in his lectures, he invited her to take one of his courses, and he sent her a copy of *Zygon: Journal of Religion and Science*, the 1973 September–December double issue consisting of papers from the Symposium on Science and Human Purpose. She read it from cover to cover, and there she learned about IRAS and the Star Island conferences.

So in 1977, Marj came to the conference titled "Aesthetics, Symbols, and Truth in Science and Religion." There she listened to Eugene d'Aquili's lecture called "The Neurobiological Bases of Myth and Concepts of Deity."[9] Gene was known for offering complex lectures with a rapid-fire presentation and big scientific words, such as the *inferior parietal lobule* of the brain. I and many others barely got the gist of what he was saying. But Marj, with her scientific training, understood it all. For her, Gene's lecture opened up in a very detailed way the question as to whether religion might be nothing but the activity of the brain. And she began to experience dissonance between the science she practiced, taught, and appreciated—and her Christian faith.

As she came out of the lecture hall for the morning coffee break, apparently the look on her face revealed to George Riggan the cognitive dissonance she was experiencing as a result of the lecture. He joined her for coffee, and in their ensuing conversation she came to realize that she could indeed hold her faith in a way that also appreciated the naturalistic thinking of neural science; she need not give up one for the other.

Was this realization a spiritual transformation? Certainly I think it was new understanding or understanding something more clearly than before. It also was a new self-understanding that integrated two aspects of Marj's own history and personality to create a new self-identity—scientist-Christian. We might regard this as an ordinary kind of spiritual transformation, the kind of spiritual transformation that can occur in any of our lives when we cross the waters, when we pass from a problem state in our lives or thought, through a liminal or threshold experience, into a new understanding of who we are. We will learn more about some ordinary spiritual transformations in the next chapter. There I invite you to consider some passages in your own life as I share with you some of my own spiritual autobiography.

3

Passages

Reading: Confronted by God

In his book, *The Struggle of the Soul*, Lewis Sherrill describes how God continually confronts us in the circumstances of our lives prompting us to grow.[1]

> At any time from infancy to old age, crises may arise in the individual life. In any one of myriad combinations of outward and inward events, one finds him or herself in circumstances where one feels the compulsion to pass over some sort of Jordan and enter some new level of responsibility and recompense. And yet this new step forward is a step into the unknown, peopled with dangerous creatures of fact, as truly as with menacing creations of fancy. The stage one has already reached in growth is good, though not yet fully satisfying. In that case is it better to bear the ills we know or to fly to others we know not of? So the motive of growth is met by the motive of shrinking back. In that time of conflict we have come into crisis, whether we are one year old or three score years and ten. . . .

. . . the garments God wears, so to speak, when confronting us very often are no other than the circumstances which confront us and which require of us a decision to grow, or to stay as we are, or to regress. It is these circumstances which compel us to decide, and these circumstances of the common life may be the form in which God comes again into our little part of human history, coming thus to our senses, confronting us, calling on us for the response of faith to the end that we may "enter in" a little further.

Again, these crises and these confrontations are not restricted to any one age or period of life. They begin in infancy, and they do not end short of the final hour of physical life.

Reflection: Passages

One of the things that I find helpful in my own reflection is looking at metaphors. In chapter 2, we looked at *crossings* as a metaphor of spiritual transformation—crossing the waters. Now I want to suggest another metaphor—*passages*. The idea of passages highlights major changes in our lives. Sometimes these passages loom up before us unexpectedly, when the circumstances in which we live suddenly change beyond our control. Our job may change as a result of new corporate leadership, an accident may disable us, a loved one may die. But there are also common passages for most people in most societies: birth, puberty, becoming a productive worker, making a marriage commitment, establishing a home, having children, retiring, dying—all are passages that involve significant transformations in how we live our lives and in who we are.

These passages are marked in many societies by religious rituals. Religious rituals recognize passages as sacred times—times in which people are expected to leave behind old ways of living—for example, leaving behind the ways of childhood in becoming an adult or giving up the ways of being single in making a life commitment to another person. Such times of transition and transformation are special periods of human becoming.

Even though the particular issues involved in a passage may vary, the key issue in all passages, according to Lewis Sherrill, is the same. Does one grow into a new phase of life or hold back? Does one respond to the challenging circumstances with faith in the future or with hanging on to what one already has and not letting go? To move through a passage with faith in the future, is, according to Sherrill, to respond to a call from God. In this chapter, I'll illustrate how Sherrill's ideas have been meaningful to me as I have gone through some of the passages in my own life. Even though I will be narrating some of my own spiritual autobiography, I hope my experiences will evoke similar experiences in your lives upon which you can reflect for yourself.

The first thing that I've experienced in life passages is that, even with faith, the times of passage are risky, scary times. We can look at how other human beings live in the stage of life we are entering and imagine new possibilities. As theologian Philip Hefner has pointed out, being in touch with the sacred is being open to new possibilities.[2] Yet, we do not really know how we will handle the new stage of life. I remember a significant passage in my own life when I asked my first wife, Carol, to marry me more than forty-five years ago. The time and place are still vivid in my mind. And so are my first thoughts when I woke up the morning after. My first thought was, "my God, what have I done?" I had a similar experience when I retired from Rollins College after twenty-eight years of teaching. Looking forward to life in retirement but recognizing that I could not really envision it, I had another "my God, what have I done" experience.

After I retired from full-time teaching, I enjoyed the amount of time I had at my disposal. More important, I felt that I was in control of my own time more than I had ever been, and I liked that. I continued to read and did a little writing. But I also enjoyed just sitting–doing nothing in particular until after a period of time I naturally felt the urge to get up, move, and start some activity that came to me that moment. It might be picking up something to read, doing a small job around the house, or getting myself something to eat. I didn't have to accomplish anything. How relaxing–no pressure!

At the same time, I did not feel quite right about this. Could I live in this low pressure, relaxed mode for the next thirty years? My underlying anxiety came to the fore when I attended a conference devoted to understanding human beings as complex systems, as personalities with many subpersonalities.[3] I liked this way of thinking about myself as a person that had many interacting parts as well as a core state of experience, which many at the conference called "being in self." This meant being in a calm, compassionate, centered state that was attentive to all parts of my internal system. In this state, I could explore my inner workings and assist the parts of me to work together to promote my own well-being and my relationships with others.

In one of the sessions I attended, conducted by two psychotherapists, we were introduced to different techniques for doing inner-work. These techniques took me into a meditative state with guiding images that allowed me to travel around in my own mind. In one exercise, after we were guided into a state of calm centeredness, we were asked to image our future. Immediately there rose up from the depths of my psyche a great black blob, locating and growing itself in my gut in a way that gave me a sinking feeling of despair and terrifying fear. Was this my future? Was all that lay ahead of me darkness and death?

As the leader of this exercise brought us out of our meditative-imaging state, I began to reflect on the meaning of what I had experienced. I realized that subconsciously I was probably grappling with

the fact that I was now retired, that I was slug-
gishly drifting from one thing to the next without
much direction. Blackness was pulling me down—
inertia was holding me back. After my career as
a teacher, I no longer had a primary governing
purpose in life.

However, as I reflected on the image of the big
black blob, recalling it back to the center of my
consciousness, I began to notice that it was not
all black. Within the blackness, there were threads
of green and blue and brown. These brought to
my mind the idea of a generative earth. Maybe
out of the darkness something new was beginning to emerge. And as I imaged this aspect of my
experience further, I saw that out of the darkness
a sun was rising. And in that sun was a face—a
face I knew well. It was the face of a one-year-old
child—the face of one of my granddaughters.

What did it all mean? It seemed I was in a process of transformation, a passage from one phase of
my life that was now ended to some other, yet not
fully defined, phase. I did not know where I was
going, but I felt I could begin to go forward—being
lead by the face of that child in the rising sun.

One way to interpret such experiences is in
terms of the ideas of Lewis Sherrill. I first read
Sherrill when I attended theological school in the
early 1960s. More than ten years later, reflecting
on what I had done there, I concluded that the
most influential book I had read was Sherrill's *The
Struggle of the Soul.* I gave it to some of my students

at Rollins College and also, in 1982 to my parents, with the following inscription: "To Mom and Dad, who have been to me examples of the life of faith written about in this book!"

The life of faith written about by Sherrill and exemplified by my parents (my father and step-mother) is one of responding to God's continual confrontations in the circumstances of our lives by being willing to let go of the stage of life we have already attained and being open to a new and largely unknown future. Sherrill sees this as how we grow spiritually as we move through the cycles of our lives. In light of this understanding, trying to hold on to the past in the midst of changing circumstances is resisting the divine. It is deny-ing the promptings of the sacred creative process to move forward, to grow into new kinds of roles and responsibilities as a mature human being. For Christians, this denial is a form of sin. It is a refusal to enter into a passage—to pass through into an unknown territory—a promised land. In contrast, faith is the ability to trust the process of transfor-mation that is occurring, to be open to being led into the new, even though unknown, good that can emerge.

This was the faith that I had seen in my par-ents. I saw it in the way my father responded to the death of my biological mother in 1952, when I was thirteen. In the midst of his grief, he became both father and mother to me—resulting in a closely woven shared life that I still treasure in my memory. And, as time passed, he became open to a new life for him and for me when in 1955 he married Alice. Dad committed to a new life-companion, and I took the leap forward by calling Alice "mother." It was an act of faith that she would become my mother, which she fully did. Mom, who was then forty-eight, had never been married. Some of her friends thought that she might be making a big mistake, marrying a man with a teenage son. But she had faith—faith in me that I would be like my father—a faith that led us to have an almost fifty-year, wonderful mother-son relationship. Mom and Dad listened to God in the circumstances of their lives. They allowed themselves to be led through a passage into a new future together. Because they were willing to leave behind the old and embrace the new, their future was a new and good life together. And I, too, benefited from a new family of aunts, uncles, and cousins.

The faith of my parents was my guiding example during the most difficult passage of my life. Just before Christmas in 1993, my wife Carol was diagnosed with a rare form of stomach cancer, a form that was judged to be untreatable by the protocols of one of the leading cancer centers in the country. This was confirmed by second and third opinions. She was given six months to live. Working with our doctors and with the help of a feeding tube inserted as her stomach ceased to function, we extended that six months to fifteen months.

The help from our doctors, the support of dear friends, and our fascinating and open exploration into complementary forms of medicine, including meditation, sustained us in what I came to think of as our medical-spiritual journey—a journey through a passage into the unknown future.

How could I find meaning in this journey into the unknown? By the end of October 1994, I found myself living our journey in terms of three metaphors. First, in keeping with our life in a college community, a life with its own annual rhythms, I began to think of Carol's dying as a graduation or commencement. This was, of course, not a graduation from school, although she and I had done that many times, but a graduation from life. It was a commencement into a new phase of being—a phase in which her ashes would be recycled through the earth while her spirit was transformed to live on in love.

A second metaphor was that our daily struggle with her illness, facing ever new health and personal challenges, was like living on a frontier. It was a frontier of mountains and valleys. We struggled up to and through high passes into new momentarily peaceful valleys, only to meet more rocky difficulties. With a realism that was not afraid of death, with a strong will to live as long as there were moments in which life still had quality, and with the support of heath care workers, family, friends, and kind strangers, we journeyed on the frontier of life and death.

Finally, a third metaphor, that of a high mountain hike, enabled me to cross a threshold and, when the time came, to let go of the one I loved. I imagined that she and I were alone in the high terrain, having left behind the others who were supporting our journey. I saw us hiking along a high ridge, above the timberline, overlooking deep valleys, looking down into the past of our lives. As the climb became more difficult—at times very painful and exhausting—we were able to see more, understand more, and love more.

Then on the left side of the ridge we came to a steep cliff wall, a wall we could not climb. As we hiked along the wall, we came to a cave. Carol explored the cave by herself. I imagined that she found a tunnel, with a shaft of smooth rock down which she could slide whenever she was ready to let go. At the end of the tunnel, I imagined a light—a symbol to me of new life that completed her spiritual transformation.

I was not ready to enter the cave and the tunnel. I was entering my own difficult spiritual transformation. When she died, I began my difficult trek—alone—back down from the mountains, from the high ridges and cliffs into the low hills and valleys of everyday life, to be together with family and friends. I had my own further passages to make, my own new frontiers to cross. But because our lives had become so interwoven during the thirty-three years of our married life, Carol, in another form—in the spirit of memory and love—has continued with me on my journey on the edge of time.

As Sherrill says, the circumstances of our lives, the way things come together, can be understood in faith to be the garment of the presence of God in our lives—a presence that in the circumstances calls us often to pass through a valley of the shadow of death to a new life with new good. The frontier spirit of Carol and the faith of my parents supported me as I came back down from the mountain into a new and unknown form of everyday life as a single, fifty-five-year-old man. It also was a faith that allowed me to be open to—yes, even hope for and act toward—a new relationship. As a result, four and a half years after Carol's death, I was blessed with a new marriage, a wonderful companion of mind and heart, and, for the first time in my life, children and grandchildren. And one of those grandchildren, Amelia—when she was just over a year old—was the face in the rising sun. It is that face in a new dawn of my life that is helping me to keep writing and speaking after I have retired from teaching. It is that face and the faces of other children in my new family that are opening all the wonderful opportunities that come with my new identity—grandpa.

So these are some of my experiences of a few major passages in my life, and some metaphors and images that have emerged in my mind to give meaning to my experiences. None of us face exactly the same crises. But all of us face a life of continually being challenged by the way things come together on the cutting edges of our lives. As we move through the passages of our lives, we all are challenged—in unexpected and sometimes unwelcome ways—to move beyond who we have been. There is a natural tendency to shrink back, to refuse the call to new possibilities in a risky and often scary future. However, if we accept the challenges to live in new and different ways, if we are able to move into new, unfolding futures, we can understand ourselves as responding to a divine call to ongoing spiritual becoming as we travel the journeys of our lives.

4

Rebirths

Reading: Born Again—The Process

This reading from Marcus Borg's book *The Heart of Christianity* describes the variety of "born-again" experiences in Christianity and other religions.[1]

> The born-again experience can be sudden and dramatic. It can involve a dramatic revelation, a life-changing epiphany, as in the case of Saul on the road to Damascus, an experience through which he became Paul. Such dramatic conversions continue to this day; some people can name a day or even an hour when it happened. There is no reason to doubt that such "sudden conversions" occur. William James not only reports many such experiences but speaks of them as one of the most remarkable psychological phenomena known. . . .
>
> But for most of us, this takes time. And even for those who can name an hour when they were born again, the process of living into the new life takes time. . . .

The born-again metaphor not only applies to a single dramatic event or a lifelong process, but also to the shorter rhythms in our lives. It is a process that may occur several times in periods of major transitions, whatever the cause.

It even applies to the micro-rhythms of daily life. . . . The "dailiness" of the process fits my experience, as it does that of many people I know. In the course of a day, I sometimes realize that I have become burdened, and that the cause is that I have forgotten God. In the act of remembering God, of reminding myself of the reality of God, I sometimes feel a lightness of being—a rising out of my self-preoccupation and burdensome confinement. We are called again and again to come forth from our tombs.

The process is at the heart not only of Christianity, but of the other enduring religions of the world. The image of following "the way" is common in Judaism, and "the way" involves a new heart, a new self centered in God. One of the meanings of the word "Islam" is "surrender": to surrender one's life to God by radically centering in God. And Muhammad is reported to have said, "Die before you die." Die spiritually before you die physically, die metaphorically (and really) before you die literally. At the heart of the Buddhist path is "letting go"—the same internal path as dying to an old way of being and being born into a new. According to the *Tao Te Ching*, a foundational text for both Taoism and Zen Buddhism, Lao Tzu said, "If you want to become full, let yourself be empty; if you want to be reborn, let yourself die."

Reflection: Rebirths

There is much talk these days about spirituality. From my experience in discussing spirituality with people, I would say that what many of us are seeking is a deepening of connections. We are seeking, first, a deepening of connections within ourselves—a sense of personal wholeness; second, a deepening of connections with others—especially emotional connections; and, third, a deepening of connections with the wider world—a feeling of being at home in the universe. Behind all this, in and through all this, I think people are seeking a connection with the sacred, with what is of greatest value and meaning within themselves, in communion with others, and in harmony with the natural world, a connection with the sacred that many call God.

In this chapter, I shall continue to explore how spirituality develops through transformative events in our lives. In the previous two chapters, I have used the metaphors of crossings and passages, and several others metaphors as well, to talk about spiritual transformation. Now I want to lift up still more metaphors. One is the Christian metaphor from the New Testament—being born again, or being born anew. Marcus Borg in *The Heart of Christianity* suggests that being born again or being born anew is not so much a matter of what we believe. Rather it is a matter of changes in our selves, in our identity, in the way we live our lives.

As we move through the passages in the cycles of our lives, we are continuously being born anew as we cross thresholds to realize new possibilities in our own living and dying. As we do this, we can experience another new birth that is even more fundamental to becoming human. It is a new birth from being a separate individual, sometimes isolated and alienated from others, to being a person who is open to the world and who exhibits compassion towards others and who is a contributing citizen to society. For some, such as the environmentalist Aldo Leopold, it is a new birth to become a citizen of the natural world—taking responsibility for acting in harmony with the rest of nature.[2]

Borg writes about this new birth using another metaphor of spiritual transformation—"opening the heart." As a biblical scholar, he says that the word "heart" occurs over one thousand times in the Bible. It most cases, it is a metaphor for the self. Biblical phrases like "Serve the Lord with all your heart," "Your law is within my heart," "Where your treasure is, there your heart will be also," and "God searches the heart"—these all are ways of expressing what we often mean by the self that is the core of our being.[3]

Borg goes on to talk of "closed hearts" and "open hearts."[4] Closed hearts are turned in on themselves and are not open to others, to the wider world, or to God. A person with a closed heart has limited vision, is self-deceptive, and lacks gratitude. A closed-hearted person is insensitive to wonder and awe, forgets nature or God as the wider source of his or her being, lacks compassion, and is insensitive to injustice.

How do closed hearts develop? I think the capacity for developing a closed heart might lie partly in our evolved biological natures. Over time, humans have evolved through natural selection to have self-protective emotions and behaviors. These have been selected to preserve and continue our genes through reproduction. Of course we also have evolved to have other emotions and behaviors that support close family relationships, especially bonding relationships between parents and children, as well as relationships of reciprocity with nonfamily—doing to others as we would have them do to us. These other-directed capacities open our hearts to others—even as we preserve and continue our genetic line. Still, under certain conditions, our self-protective emotions and behaviors can take over and isolate us from others and the wider world.

In part, the development of closed hearts may be an aspect of normal human growth and of neurological and psychological development. When as children we develop self-awareness, we come to experience ourselves as separated from others. Furthermore, when we feel excessively criticized, humiliated, hurt, abandoned, and abused, we dissociate from others and even from other parts of ourselves.

Sometimes during a passage in our life cycle, something happens that holds us back, that increases our separateness and isolation. In my own life, when I went through puberty, I experienced the dying of my first mother over a period of two-and-a-half years. As I look back on that time of my life, I remember that my friends were beginning to engage in early teenage social life, and my best friend fell in love and spent most of his time with his girlfriend. But the crisis in our family kept me more at home, often by myself. I now can say that my heart became more closed as I became more withdrawn and wrapped up in myself. I continued to do well in my studies, but I did not reach out to have the kind of interactions that a part of me craved, but another part of me was afraid to engage in.

In contrast to the closed heart, Borg describes an open heart as seeing things more clearly, being alive to wonder, to the sheer marvel of "isness." "An open heart and gratitude go together." Borg suggests that "we can feel this in our bodies. In the moments in my life when I have been most grateful, I have felt a swelling, almost a bursting, in my chest."[5]

In those who have "an open heart," compassion and a passion for justice go together. An open heart feels the suffering and pain of the world and responds to it. Compassion and a passion for justice are the ethical impulse and imperative that go with an open heart. "'Be compassionate as God is compassionate,' Jesus said."[6] Borg concludes this part of his book by saying that "the Christian life is about a new heart, an open heart, a heart of flesh, a heart of compassion."[7] I think that the Buddha, in his own way, would agree. So would many who are not traditionally religious. Spirituality is about developing connectedness that is grounded in compassion for others. To develop such an open heart is to be born anew—to be spiritually transformed.

How does one go through a transformation process to become more open hearted? In the previous chapter, I suggested that life passages are often initiated by challenging circumstances, which in Sherrill's words are the "garment of God."[8] Now, following Borg, I'd like to introduce another metaphor—*thin places*. "Thin places" is a Celtic Christian metaphor for coming in contact with the sacred, which is present all around and in and through us, but which often is hidden from us. This idea about the immanence of the sacred reminds me of what the French Jesuit paleontologist Teilhard de Chardin called the "divine milieu" in the title of one of his books—the divine environment.[9] It's always there, but, in a few instances, in thin places, it becomes manifest in our lives more clearly and effectively.

Borg says that "a thin place is anywhere our hearts are opened," or opened up again, opened up more.[10] Nature, especially wild nature or the panorama of the stars, can be a thin place. In her book, *Sacred Depths of Nature*, cell biologist Ursula Goodenough talks about how her scientific research brings her to a sense of awe, gratitude, and responsibility for other human beings and our planet. We might say her science brings her to thin places.[11]

Rituals, yoga, and other kinds of meditation can become thin places. So can nonreligious music, poetry, literature, the visual arts, and dance. I remember one experience I had while dancing. I'm not much of a dancer, but some years ago I took ballroom dancing lessons. After a few years, I became reasonably average. And there were a few special moments. One was when I was reviewing some steps to the waltz with my instructor. As I began to put it all together, it didn't matter that we were in a cleared section of a school cafeteria. It didn't matter that we were listening to taped music. I began the waltz with the usual box step, moved to a twinkle and then to double and triple twinkles, and still other advanced steps. And we began to move in perfect time with the music around the floor—again and again—becoming one with the music, flowing in the experience of the waltz. It became, indeed, what some call a "flow" experience. I felt like I was opening up into another dimension of life experience which left me emotionally breathless—and with deep gratitude for what my instructor had enabled me to do and experience.

People can become thin places: religious founders such as the Buddha, Jesus, Mohammed, Handsome Lake of the Iroquois. People like Gandhi, Mother Theresa, Martin Luther King Jr.—

remember his "I Have a Dream" speech. Small children also can be thin places. Over the past three years, I have watched two grandchildren grow in a wondrous process from infants in my arms, to crawling, to standing, to toddling, to beginning to talk. As their brain neurons and body muscles organize themselves in the miracle of human development, I experience wonder and gratitude for the gift of life we all have. I experience a thin place.

Another human being who was a thin place for me was a man I met in Hong Kong while I was at a graduate student seminar, circa 1970. One of the aims of our seminar was to meet with university students to discuss world affairs as they were related to our lives. On an afternoon at the University of Hong Kong, about fifteen students from the United States met with the same number of students from Hong Kong. At that meeting was a slightly older man—not a student—but one who was working to unite the working people of the city to better their labor conditions.

It became clear to me that he was a charismatic leader for these students. I, too, felt the power of his personality and his vision. I learned that he had written a number of pamphlets related to his labor organizing activity. After the meeting, I talked with him, and told him that some day I would probably be reading his work in the United States. "Oh no," he replied. "I'm not interested in writing for the world. I'm only interested in my work here in Hong Kong. That is enough." His words and their significance had a powerful effect on me: it is better to focus on doing good work in a smaller sphere of influence than trying to become known to the wider world. In this way, he became for me a thin place.

Thin places can also be places of worship. One of my most memorable worship experiences took place on Star Island at a conference of the Institute on Religion in an Age of Science (IRAS). At the highest point on the island stands a small stone chapel. Each night on Star Island the conference day closes with a simple candlelight service. Conferees carry candle lanterns from the porch of the hotel up the path to the chapel. Once inside, they hang the lanterns on sconces, bathing the chapel in its only source of light. It's a beautiful setting.

One time in the early 1970s, the Star Island chapel became for me a thin place. The conference had been a wonderful week of exciting ideas and meaningful conversations. I felt good as I walked up the path to the chapel in silence, carrying my lantern. Ahead of me, I noticed that some were looking north at the sky. When I turned, I saw the most magnificent display of northern lights I had ever seen. In the chapel, I sat in the back corner. As was customary in those days at our religion and science conference, the Friday night candlelight was a Jewish Shabbat service, conducted by Rabbi Jerome Molino and his wife Rhoda Molino from Danbury, Connecticut. The service was all in Hebrew. I did not understand a word. But as I sat in this candle-lit stone chapel, listing to the sacred sounds of the service, something came over me. I can't describe it. The whole week, the aurora borealis, the chapel all came together in an absolutely thrilling way. I sat there in silence, tingling, emotionally moved to tears at the beauty of what I felt. Today, I would say that I was experiencing a thin place.

I've had that same experience often in the sanctuary of my church, the Unitarian Society of Hartford. You may have had this experience in places where you worship. When I enter the sanctuary of my church on Sunday morning, its design and the lighting makes me aware that I'm in a special place—a sacred space. When I experience greetings from others, hear the music of organ and choir, sing the hymns, and close my eyes to flow with the words of a prayerful reflection, a reading, or a sermon, I often find myself moved to tears—my ego dissolving as my heart opens up to memories of those gone but still dear to me, as I open up to hearing the needs of those who are suffering, as I'm called and guided to connect with the wider reality that is the source of my being and of the meaning in my life.

So thin places can occur in worship, in nature, in art, music, and dance, through people, and in our interactions with one another. When they happen, we become more centered in the sacred. We experience rebirth, being "born again" as our hearts open up to new possibilities as we travel forward in our lives on the edge of time. As our hearts open up more fully to one another in love, we become more human. We become more connected within ourselves, with others, with the wider world. We grow in spirituality.

.

5

Conversion

Reading: Being Converted

In his classic work *The Varieties of Religious Experience*, William James opens his chapter, "Conversion," with the following: [1]

> To be converted, to be regenerated, to receive grace, to experience religion, to gain assurance, are so many phrases which denote the process, gradual or sudden, by which a self hitherto divided, and consciously wrong[,] inferior[,] and unhappy, becomes unified and consciously right superior and happy, in consequence of its firmer hold upon religious realities. This at least is what conversion signifies in general terms, whether or not we believe that a direct divine operation is needed to bring such a moral change about.

Reflection: Conversion

Another way to reflect on the movement from closed to open hearts is to consider that the transformation involved is one of conversion.

Conversion is a common Christian term for signaling a fundamental reorientation of a person from living apart from God to living with the sacred as the center of one's being. Philosopher of religion John Hick says that conversion is a transformation from self-centeredness to God-centeredness or Reality-centeredness.[2] Another way to understand conversion is from a state of being fragmented and dysfunctional to a state of being whole, as William James suggests. This can be extended to relationships among humans—from dysfunctional families to well-functioning families, for example. And it can even include the transformation of humans from a state of being in conflict with other creatures and the natural world to living in harmony with nature in a peaceable kingdom. The understandings of Hick and James are not opposed to each other. They can be combined when one recognizes that being in a state of God-centeredness results in personal integration and harmonious dynamic relations with others. When one is "in God" one moves from a dysfunctional state to a state of functioning well. Conversion is the process by which one is transformed from ordinary and often fragmented living into a state of being centered in the sacred or holy.

For me, one of the most helpful ways to develop this understanding of conversion is the thinking of psychologist Richard C. Schwartz. To help us understand ourselves, Schwartz has developed a view called "internal family systems" thinking.

This kind of thinking suggests that each of us is a system containing subpersonalities or parts.[3] This is analogous to thinking about a family as a system of interacting persons. Just as families contain persons that may live more or less well together, so an individual contains parts that may be in tension or conflict with one another or, on the other hand, may work effectively together in a well-coordinated, well-functioning person.

Let's explore Schwartz's idea in a little more detail. The core of a person is what he calls the *self*. It is the state of being centered in the sacred that I mentioned above; we might also say that it is being in our sacred center. In various religious traditions, it has been called soul, essence, spirit, mind of Christ, Buddha nature, *atman* (Hinduism), Jiva (Jainism), and God consciousness. I find it helpful to regard this self or sacred center not as a thing but as a state of being that is manifest in a felt experience. It is a state in which we are in the present moment. We are calm and centered, peaceful yet energized. We are confident, curious, creative, and compassionate. In this state, we are understanding and not judging. We are connecting and not disengaging, healing and not hurting. In traditional Christian terms, we might say we are in a state called *salvation*.

Besides what Schwartz calls our *self*, we also have parts. Other psychologists have developed views of the human personality as consisting of parts. Sigmund Freud speaks of the id, ego, and superego. Carl Jung talks about such archetypes as the persona, shadow, anima, and animus. And James suggests that our "ideas, aims, and objects form diverse internal groups and systems, relatively independent of one another."[4]

Drawing on several years of counseling practice, Schwartz suggests that we have three major kinds of parts: exiles, managers, and firefighters, based on how they function in our inner system.[5] Exiles are the parts we experience when we are feeling sad, afraid, hurt, rejected, worthless, powerless, and ashamed, when we are feeling hopeless, empty, and unlovable. I've had feelings like these. These are the kind of feelings we don't like to feel. We want to hide them, to put them into a closet. Hence, they are called exiles.

Managers are parts that, often in response to the feelings we want to exile, try to keep order and control. Sometimes they do this by trying to be perfect, pleasing, and caretaking of others. Sometimes managers do this by being judgmental and critical of others and ourselves. Sometimes they keep control by intellectualizing, rationalizing, and denying.

However, when our managers can't keep control, and exiled feelings come pouring out and threaten to overwhelm us, another kind of part steps in— a firefighter. Firefighters try to help the person regain control by extinguishing painful feelings or by disconnecting a person from them with alcohol, drugs, food binges, sex binges, shopping binges, too much sleep, rage and violence, clinical depression, and suicidal thinking.

Where do all these parts come from? I think that some of them are rooted in biological predispositions that have been naturally selected in the evolution of our species to help us survive and reproduce. For example, many of our exiles have a basis in fear. Fear can be a good thing, a warning signal that something is threatening us. The feeling of fear is located in specific regions of our brains, involving specific neural circuits and specific neural transmitters. As we grow up, these circuits may get connected to certain threatening experiences, say the criticism of parents or their threat to withdraw care and love. Humans have evolved with genetic predispositions for parent-child bonding—especially mother-child bonding—because of the long period of child dependency before self-sufficiency. Therefore, the threat of parental withdrawal from a child is very likely to evoke fear.[6]

Likewise, anger can be an appropriate response when we are threatened by others. It warns us that something is wrong, and it warns others to back off. Like fear, anger appears to be naturally selected, genetically programmed into certain brain circuits with certain neurotransmitters. And, like fear, these circuits carrying anger can be reinforced by events in our life histories and triggered by current events.[7]

Two quite different events in my life illustrate these examples of fear and anger and the idea of internal parts described by Schwartz's model. One is from my childhood. My parents were wonderful parents in many ways. Among other things, they encouraged me to grow and to think freely for myself. Yet, like most parents, they occasionally had to discipline me. A common mode of discipline was to separate me from them. They sent me to my room without supper. On car trips, when I really acted up, they would stop the car and threaten to leave me on the side of the road.

This was so traumatic that I once dreamed about it. One of the earliest dreams I remember began with our getting ready to go somewhere. I was dawdling, slow to get ready. Suddenly my parents were not there. I rushed to the window and saw them driving away in our family car. To this day I have a part of myself—a little child part— that is afraid of being abandoned by those closest to me. When I'm in that state of fear, I feel that things are out of control, and I am sinking into a deep state of helplessness.

I have also found that a feeling of helplessness and being-out-of-control can happen with people who push my buttons. I remember a student who was especially bright and who would eventually go to graduate school. She was a free spirit, who held strong opinions and who argued them force- fully. They were very good opinions. But when she got going, she dominated the class discussion, and others had a difficult time participating.

When this happened, I found that my managers would try to keep control of her and the class. And when they were not successful, I would experience anger welling up inside me. A firefighter was being engaged. I would begin to argue back—feeling aggressive and angry—trying to shut her up. But that didn't help much; she only became more assertive.

So, I found myself in a state of inner conflict. A part of me was angry, but another part knew that being angry was not helping. I also had feelings of inadequacy. I was supposedly a good teacher. How could I be letting this happen? I was in a state that James calls a divided self, a person who is "divided, and consciously wrong inferior and unhappy." In contrast, I wanted to feel "unified and consciously right superior and happy."[8] Not right and superior in the sense of being morally superior and dominant over others but in the sense of functioning well, with all my parts working together. I wanted to feel like I was in a state of self-leadership. And I also wanted to feel that I was an effective, facilitative leader with my students.

Using Schwartz's model, I suggest that the way in which our conflicting parts can become transformed, so that states like fear and anger can work constructively together, is to undergo conversion into a state of being in *self*, to being in our sacred center, to living in the spirit of God. How do we move from a state of divided personality with extreme and conflicting parts into a state of being in our sacred center?

The conversion process as studied by many scholars is complex. Much of the recent work that has scientifically studied conversion is summarized in Lewis Rambo's book *Understanding Religious Conversion*.[9] Rambo sees a number of factors involved in a person's conversion: cultural, societal, personal, and religious factors. Cultural factors, studied, for example, by anthropologists, may include a society's ways of speaking and thinking, and its values and ideals. Often these are expressed in stories about the origins and destinies of its people, what scholars call the myths of the society. A myth connects a description of the way things are with the norms by which people live. Right now, we are thinking in terms of a modern myth. The story underlying my use of Schwartz's internal family systems model of the person is an evolutionary story. Our parts and our core self are biopsychological phenomena that help us function well as dynamically integrated individuals in mutually supportive relations with other humans and the wider natural world. Embodied in this story are the values of wholeness and harmonious life in loving relationships.

Societal factors refer to the institutions of the society that embody the culture. For me, in our pluralistic society, these include my church community, an academic community of people in science and religion, religious studies, and philosophy, as well as a community that engages in pastoral counseling or psychotherapy. I think you may find yourselves in similar communities that provide resources for guiding a quest to become transformed from a fragmented, alienated person to one who is able to lead all of his or her parts in effective relationships with others.

Continuing to follow the thinking of Rambo on the factors that influence conversion, we can also highlight a religious component, which I already have described as our sacred center, the divine or holy that is present as the core of our being, which Christians might call *image of God.* This sacred center also extends far beyond us as the creative source of all that is. The idea of the sacred expresses what we think has the greatest value, that which is worthy of being the center of our lives. Some think of this as a being that is creative, caring, compassionate, and connected with all that is. When they become converted to a life centered in God, they feel that they have entered into a loving relationship with such a being. In my own religious living, I find it helpful to think of the sacred center as a state in which I can be, as a process in which I can participate. I think of God in human life as a dynamic state of calm, compassionate, courageous, and caring creativity, in which I can live in a process of human becoming.

Rambo's final factor of conversion is the personal dimension. That is what I've been exploring, following the opening reading from James. So the question is, how do the cultural, societal, and religious components of conversion all come together to transform someone like me from a person who is fearful of being isolated, and who gets upset and angry, into someone who can calmly live effectively in relation to others?

Let's return to the model of transformation suggested by Victor Turner, which we first discussed in chapter 2, to help explore the process by which conversion takes place. I suggest that the first step is a deeply felt dissatisfaction with the way one is—the unhappiness that James mentions. An example of such a state might be what some Christians call a *conviction of sin*, a deep remorse about the way one is living. Buddhists see it as a recognition that suffering is caused by clinging to what is constantly changing, grounded in a dualistic ignorance that there is this and that, I and you. Another example might be when a person seeks help from a psychotherapist because of dissatisfaction with his or her behaviors, thoughts, or feelings.

Continuing to follow Turner, a second step is attempting to distance oneself from the way one has been. Seeking therapy may be a part of this. So might going to revival meetings, or engaging in new religious practices with others or by oneself. In my own case, I have learned to quiet myself down, to center myself by simply taking deep breaths. Breathing to relax is a simple but often effective way to move from a state of agitation and confusion into a state of relaxed centeredness.

Such breathing can become a form of meditation. The Buddhist monk Thich Nhat Hanh gives us a way that helps us to enter into a centered state, called in Buddhist terms *mindfulness*. When we are mindful, we are present fully to ourselves and to others. He says "conscious breathing is the most basic Buddhist practice for touching peace" and he offers this short exercise. "Breathing in, I calm my body. Breathing out, I smile. Dwelling in the present moment, I know this is a wonderful moment." He then shortens this to: "As we breathe in, we say to ourselves 'Calming,' And as we breathe out, we say 'Smiling.' As we breath in again, we say, 'Present moment,'" and as we breath out, 'Wonderful moment.'"[10] As you read this, I suggest you try it!

As we enter into such practices, we may come to what Turner calls a *liminal* point, a threshold, a passage into a new way of being. One way to enter into such a passage is to simply let go! I can't say how often I have been in situations where I find a motto from Alcoholics Anonymous helpful: "Let go, Let God." Stop relying on yourself, and trust the wider reality in which you live and move and have your being. Another way is to accept Jesus into your heart and trust in him to guide your living. However one conceives of this, whether as a higher power, the presence of Christ, or the Buddha nature, this letting go and trusting resources beyond oneself opens up a new way of being— being fully in the present moment, attentive to all that is taking place, accepting all parts of oneself, and loving others.

Occasionally religious practices that enable letting go can produce a rare form of experience that psychiatrist Eugene d'Aquili, calls "absolute unitary being," the state of oceanic consciousness described by many mystics.[11] Huston Smith, a Methodist Christian and a scholar of world religions, describes how he came to such an experience. [12] When he was interviewed by Bill Moyers for a video series *The Wisdom of Faith with Huston Smith*, Smith recounted how Buddhist practice enables him to enter in to the "deeper mind." When he was thirty-seven, he entered a Rinzai Zen Buddhist monastery in Japan for eight weeks of training. This involved eight hours of meditation a day, along with daily visits to the Roshi, the abbot of the monastery. On his second day, Smith received from the Roshi his *koan*. In Rinzai Zen, a *koan* is a meditation problem that is impossible to solve by the rational mind. However, continuous meditation on a *koan*, along with the guidance of the Zen Master, can lead to a rare, mystical experience.

There are three standard *koans*: What is the sound of one hand clapping? What was the appearance of your face before your parents were born? And the one which Smith himself received, the following story: A monk asked Joshu (who was a Zen Master back in China) "Does a dog have a Buddha nature?" To which Joshu replied, "*mu*," the Japanese word for "no." What makes this a conundrum like the first two *koans* is that all Buddhists know that even grass has a Buddha nature. So certainly dogs must also have a Buddha nature. But the answer in the *koan* is *mu*—no! Smith was sent from his Roshi to meditate on this *koan*.

At first, Smith tried redefining the meaning of the terms. Then he attempted even more ingenious solutions to present to the Roshi. The Roshi replied with a roar: "You have the philosopher's disease!" Then, more quietly, the Roshi explained that there was nothing wrong with philosophy; he himself had a master's degree in philosophy. But philosophy deals with reason, and reason can work only with the experience that it has to work with. Smith was told: "You obviously have the reason. You do not have the experience. For these weeks, put reason aside and go for the experience."

Smith explains to Moyers that the answer to these early *koans* is not a verbal answer. It is an experience. These are conundrums that present a contradiction before which reason is helpless. The Roshi kept emphasizing *mu*: "nothing but *mu*, the whole universe nothing but *mu*." Smith says that this worked as kind of mantra within him. Having knocked out the logical, rational process, Smith says that with continued concentration "at some point something gives, and you enter into the deep mind—with a kind of detonative experience. It's the mystical experience."

And so it went for Smith until the final week, when the monks meditated twenty-four hours a day. Because he was older, Smith was allowed to have three-and-a-half hours of sleep. Finally, on the second to the last day Smith was not only exhausted, but his mind was worked up into such a state that he was furious. He felt that what was being demanded was abusive. While he did not justify his anger, it was how he felt. So at his next meeting with the Roshi, he stormed into the room in an utter rage and ready to let him have it, determined not only to throw in the towel on the whole eight weeks but to throw it right in the Roshi's face. In the usual routine, he sank down on his haunches and bowed to the Roshi the customary bow. Their eyes met and the Roshi said, "How's it going?" Smith said, "The words sounded like a taunt to me, and I answered, 'terrible!!'" Then the Roshi looked at him, "You think you're going to get sick, don't you?" "Yes, I think I'm going to get sick," Smith yelled. He felt his throat closing in on him, so he could hardly breathe. Then, all of a sudden in the most objective, quiet voice imaginable, the Roshi said, "What is sickness? What is health? Put them both aside and go forward."

"And now I despair," Smith tells Moyers, "of communicating to you the effect of those words on me. Immediately with no thought, I found bubbling up in me, 'By God he's right.' And the way [I went in], sailing in with my anger, with those words he just spun me around into a state of total tranquility and peace. And I did my bow to the floor. I got up leaving the room not only determined to finish the two days . . . but knowing

I could do it." Smith says that he experienced a transfusion of energy from the Roshi to himself as he said, "By God, he's right. The opposites, sickness and health, both are irrelevant." He thought that in a normal state of mind, of course, they were different, but in that moment, he experienced that there was no difference between them.

As Smith continues to tell Moyers about this experience, he says that, as remarkable as it is, such experiences are not the real core of Zen. The real core of Zen is the subsequent hard work day after day, plodding footstep after plodding footstep, in order to bring the glow of this experience back into the nitty-gritty of daily life. Smith quotes the Zen Master Hakuin, "My daily life is no different, except that there is no conflict. Drawing water, hewing wood, in everything no obstruction, this is the mysterious happening. This is the wondrous incomparable power."

I think we can see how Smith provides an example of the insights of Rambo and Turner about conversion or spiritual transformation. In the context of the Buddhist culture of belief and values, one can talk about a problem state, which Buddhists frame as the problem of suffering that results from dualistic thinking and attachment. There is sickness and health, and we are supposed to be healthy. Then, in the social institution of the monastery, one goes through a process of distancing from daily life and seeking the help of a Master. The training under the guidance of the

Master brings a person to a threshold, to a liminal, transformative experience, in which a person enters the "deep mind," experiences a union of opposites, and becomes one with Buddha nature. Finally, one returns to daily life transformed, free of conflict, with a new kind of enabling power, out of which one lives in compassionate service to all forms of life.

In my own more modest efforts of spiritual quest, I find that dissatisfaction with the way I am, engaging in distancing practices, and finally letting go, take place over and over again. I am more like Marcus Borg when he says that throughout his day he is continually drawn back to God. In my experience, I find that at almost any moment I can take a deep breath, reorient myself into the present moment, and become mindful of all that is happening within and around me. In this way, I keep circling back to my sacred center, and, over months and years, this leads to a spiraling growth in spirituality, a more constant state of being in *self*, less inner conflict, and more effective living.

Let's return now to the examples that I gave earlier using Schwartz's internal family systems model. As I've continued a gradual form of religious conversion in the course of my life, I've discovered that I can regularly return to a state of centeredness in which I am aware of all my parts. And I can love them. I let feelings of love flood through me to my anxious child part who is afraid of being left alone. I let feelings of love go to my managers who are trying to keep me going. And I express feelings of appreciation to my firefighters—even my angry firefighter—who are trying to help me cope. But I also remind them that I am the leader—I myself—the calm, compassionate, creative state that is my sacred center. And I tell them to relax. We are all okay.

One thing in particular that I have done is to name my childlike part that is afraid of being abandoned. I call this part "Freddie." When I am in a calm, centered sate, I psychologically reach down and bring Freddie up to sit on my shoulder. In my mind I let him know that we are together. On my shoulder, he can watch as we do all kinds of interesting things—the two of us, like father and son. We read good books. Take a walk. Go out by ourselves. Write a difficult letter. Prepare a sermon. Write a chapter in a book. "I won't let you go, Freddie," my calm self, my sacred center, says. "I'll stay with you. Together we will take care of one another." When I do that, I find that my feelings of loneliness and my fears of being abandoned subside. I don't need to try to control them. Schwartz says that healing comes when we access the healing power—the effective leadership of being in our own centered self or spirit and its compassionate energy. When I am in my sacred center, I feel the tensions and conflicts between my parts diminish. I feel whole.

Being in this state also affects our relationships with others. Even as we cherish ourselves we also can cherish others, even their parts. This is what I found myself doing with the student that was pushing my buttons, making me angry and argumentative. Taking a deep and calming breath, I went into a state of centeredness and began to let loving feelings emerge in me and toward all those in my class—including the talkative student. It's hard to explain what happened. But when I was in *self*, I was able to respond in ways that showed that I cared for her and for what she was saying. This helped her to calm down, and others were able to become a part of the discussion. I then found experiential confirmation that when we are calm and centered, peaceful yet energized, curious, compassionate, and fully present in the moment for others, then healing occurs—not only within ourselves but also in troublesome relationships with others.

Being in a calm, centered state in the present moment is a way to love others. Thich Nhat Hanh writes: "When we are mindful, touching deeply the present moment, we can see and listen deeply, and the fruits are always understanding, acceptance, love, and the desire to relieve suffering and bring joy. When our beautiful child comes up to us and smiles, we are completely there for her."[13] In another place he writes: "The most precious gift we can offer others is our presence. When our mindfulness embraces those we love, they will bloom like flowers. If you love someone but rarely make yourself available to him or her, that is not true love. . . . When you are really there, showing your loving-kindness and understanding, the energy of the Holy Spirit is with you."[14] We might also say that the Buddha nature is in us, that we are in a state the Hindus call *atman*, and Christians call *having the mind of Christ*. Or we might say with Richard Schwartz, "We are in self." We are in our sacred center—having undergone a conversion from, as James says, being "divided, and consciously wrong interior and unhappy" to becoming "unified and consciously right superior and happy."

6

Callings

Reading: Serendipitous Creativity

In this passage from my book, *Dancing with the Sacred*, I describe Harvard theologian Gordon Kaufman's idea of the divine as serendipitous creativity.[1]

Serendipitous creativity points to dynamic and ever-changing systems, the parts of which work together in unpredictable ways to create such things as new life, new truth, and new community. We can use the idea of serendipitous creativity to talk about the religious significance of biological evolution or of the birth and development of a single living organism. Various components come together in unpredictable ways to create a new species and also new individuals. For example, the interactions of our genes, our family environment, our wider society, and our natural world work together to make each of us a unique human being. . . .

We also can use the idea of serendipitous creativity to talk about progress in science. If one reads James Watson's book *The Double Helix*, one can see how serendipitous creativity describes a process of discovery in which such things as experimental facts, competing scientists, and human imagination interacted to give rise to the discovery of the structure of DNA.[2] No one fact, no one scientist, no one act of thought produced the discovery. Many of these coming together resulted in one of the major scientific discoveries of the twentieth century.

Serendipitous creativity is also a way of understanding how human communities are created.... For example, Gordon Kaufman writes that the professional community of "modern science has certainly been a human creation, but no individual or group at the time of its origins in the seventeenth century had any notion of the complex institutional structures, modes of education and discipline, moral and communal commitments, financial and physical resources, not to say ways of thinking ... which constitute science today."[3] The same is the case with modern democratic governments. No one person simply thought out and produced the complex political systems we have today. Many individuals contributed to their evolution over time, but no one could have planned or predicted their contemporary manifestations. It is the same with the building of cities. "Any modern city is the product of human planning and intention—every brick was laid by a deliberate human act, but no one simply decided modern London or New York or Tokyo would be a fine thing to build, worked out the plans, and then brought it into being."[4]

Reflection: Callings

In the two previous chapters, I considered spiritual transformation in terms of basic transformations of persons from closed to open hearts and from a state of unhappiness and conflict to one of being whole and centered in self. Now I would like to reflect on a more particular form of spiritual transformation, that of "callings," and I'd also like to reflect more on how spiritual transformations might come about.

There are famous examples of callings such as the call of Moses at the burning bush and the call of Muhammad in the caves—the call to "recite" that created the Qur'an. I'll use a simple and more at-home experience, my own experience of a calling that I refer to on page two of my book, *Dancing with the Sacred*. I first wrote this paragraph in a class called "Writing Your Spiritual Autobiography" at my church. Here's what I wrote: "I grew up a liberal Christian, was a youth leader in my local church, had a religious experience that called me to the Christian ministry, was a fundamentalist, evangelical Christian in college, was first in my class at seminary, studied ecumenical theology in Germany, and enrolled in the Ph.D. program at Columbia University and Union Theological Seminary in New York City. By my second year in graduate school, I discovered I was an atheist."

Among other things, the book then describes how I grew out of atheism into a form of religious naturalism called *naturalistic theism.* It also describes how I developed a social-ecological understanding of the human person. Finally, *Dancing with the Sacred*, suggests how we might deal with the problem of suffering and how the intertwining of suffering and joy, and death and life, works together.

But nowhere in the book do I talk about the religious experience in 1955 that called me to Christian ministry. In fact, I never told anyone about it until January of 2003. The reason I never told anybody is simply that it was too embarrassing. However, in January 2003, I had been invited back to Rollins College, after I had retired, to give some lectures on science and religion and to visit some classes. I attended my colleague Yudit Greenberg's class on science and religion. Because the class had read parts of *Dancing with the Sacred*, I simply said that I would happy to respond to any questions about what I had written—or anything else in religion and science. Yudit smiled, what appeared to me to be a mischievous smile, and asked, "What was that religious experience you refer to on page two of your book?"

Well, I was stuck and, then, decided on the spur of the moment that maybe this was an appropriate place to reveal it, that maybe undergraduate college students would have some resonance with what I had done and experienced, because the experience occurred when I was sixteen years old.

It was an experience in which I had challenged God. I had prayed very fervently and deeply: "God, if you exist, give me a girlfriend!"

I was getting ready to attend a church camp on an island in the middle of a lake in central Wisconsin, called Camp Onaway, a Presbyterian church camp where I had been going for four years. But, when I was sixteen, I had decided not to go. Then my minister got me a scholarship from my church, which I felt I could not turn down. So, if I had to go, I felt I should get something in return. I wanted God to give me a girlfriend.

As I mentioned in chapter 4, my best friend had a girlfriend, actually had had a girlfriend for two years and had broken up with her by that time. But my mother's illness and death had kept me somewhat socially isolated in my early teen years.

Well, at the camp I got more than I asked for. First, there was Judy, who became my first girlfriend. Then I was elected president of the camp. As president, I had some responsibilities. One was to take part in the Friday evening chapel service in a lovely outdoor chapel in the woods overlooking the lake—a service in which campers were expected to dedicate their lives to Christ. As president, I was to give the Scripture reading.

The afternoon before the service, we were asked to fill out forms, asking if we wanted to commit ourselves to Christian ministry. Now, I had been filling out vocational forms since I began junior high school. The way I filled them out was related to the two influential men in my life. One was my father, who was a mechanical engineer. I liked what he did, and he took me on trips to show me firsthand what he did. So when I first began to fill out these vocational forms, I decided to follow in my father's footsteps, and I put down "engineer."

Another significant influence in my life was my minister. He encouraged me to become a minister, and he modeled what it was like to be a minister. This began to create a tension within me, so that, in succeeding years, I ended up putting down "engineer or minister." I felt some dissonance in doing this, but that's what I did when I filled out the form at Camp Onaway.

At the service, I stood up to give the Bible reading. Before I began, I looked out at my fellow campers. Suddenly I knew what I was to become. I said to myself: "This is where I belong." It was as if I had crossed a threshold in self-identity, in my understanding of what I was to become. The next morning, I met with the ministers at the camp, and told them of my decision. When they asked why, I said that I wanted to work with people. I wanted to help people.

How does one understand how such a life-transforming experience comes about? My first understanding was the one I had when I was sixteen. Then I understood that God—a personal God who hears prayers—responded to my challenge of asking for a girlfriend, but had used my challenge to call me to do the work of God. My life was changed.

But, as you have read in the above paragraph from my spiritual autobiography, by my second year in graduate school, I was an atheist. I no longer could regard this event as a call from a personal God—even though it has been one of the most important determining events of my life, and even though I still was committed to the result of that event, the call to ministry, committed to a life of helping others. How was I then to understand it? I couldn't ignore it. I had to make some sense of it.

In my graduate school studies, as I read some of the literature in psychology and other social sciences, and in American philosophy—John Dewey, in particular—I became aware of models of the process by which human beings solved problems and resolved conflicts.[5] One model suggested that when a problem or dilemma occurs, our minds work on the problem. They struggle with it—until they can't struggle anymore. Then our conscious mind lets go, and we enter into what is called an "incubation period." Here the subconscious mind is allowed to carry out its work more effectively until we suddenly reach a resolution of the problem—often in a "peak experience." And the problem is solved, or resolved. The solution is then applied, and one enters a new way of thinking, acting, or living.[6]

My problem from this perspective was complex. There was the girlfriend part of the problem. There was the vocational part of the problem—engineer or minister. And there was also a religious conflict that grew out of my mother's illness and death.

Two days after my tenth birthday, I learned that my mother was gravely ill. She began to develop a progressive yellowing in her nails, eyes, and skin. Later, I learned that this was the result of her liver failing, the result of hepatitis. As she struggled with her disease for three-and-a-half years, I prayed to God that she would become well again, that our family life would return to normal, and that my dream of having evening picnics once again on the shore of Long Lake would be fulfilled.

On December 11, 1952, she died. My prayers had not been answered. And so my challenge to God—"if you exist"—was not just trying to get a girlfriend. It was giving God a last chance—one last chance—to answer a prayer in a way that granted me an important, deep-felt wish. Just as I felt that my prayer for my mother's recovery to health was a legitimate wish, I felt that a normal teenage boy's request for a girlfriend was also legitimate.

Looking back on this with my graduate school conflict-resolution model, I saw my desperate challenge as a way of letting go, of opening up to letting my subconscious mind work on the nest of problems in my adolescent identity crisis. And my subconscious mind produced the result at that Friday evening chapel service: "This is where I belong."

As the years went by, I began to think that this internal conflict-resolution model didn't sufficiently account for all that was going on, because it leaves out the external events that also were a part of my experience, a part of my calling. It leaves out my minister and why and how he got a scholarship to send me to the camp. It leaves out a girl who also was interested in me. It leaves out the dynamics of the camp that somehow elected me to become camp president. I began to realize that my calling to ministry was also influenced by what other people did, not just by what was going on inside me.

So I developed a third understanding of how my calling came about, an understanding that has been called "serendipitous creativity." The reading for this chapter, following Gordon Kaufman's idea of *serendipitous creativity*, suggests that serendipitous creativity occurs when things come together in a way that no one can predict, and the result is something good. In the process of serendipitous creativity, human beings do intentional acts for their own reasons. Things happen in the wider world because of natural causes. In serendipitous creativity, these things all come together to create some kind of new good. What I've been describing can be considered a process in which a variety of actions by people, a church camp setting, and my own internal struggles came together in such a way as to bring about a new direction in a teenage boy's life, a new identity for that boy.

Which understanding as to how this came about do I hold today? Well, there's a part of me—an intellectual part, a rational empirical part—that tries to understand things in terms of a scientific worldview, a naturalistic worldview, if you will. With this part of me, in various papers and in the book *Dancing with the Sacred,* I've been developing a Darwinian model of serendipitous creativity. New possibilities for living are generated—for me two vocational possibilities and the possibilities elsewhere in my conflict. Those possibilities interact with one another and with other events in an environment until one of them becomes selected.[7] So with this understanding of dynamic interactions creating new possibilities, and then further interactions selecting one to continue, I can say that my experience was the result of things coming together naturally in my life, the result of "dancing with the sacred."

Another part of me likes to ask, what are the practical consequences of such a viewpoint? For me, the practical consequence is that I have begun to look for new possibilities for good in the way things come together in my living, and I also guard against possibilities that might lead to harm.

Besides my rational, empirical, naturalistic part, there is another part of me that seems more intuitive—one that experiences the world through feelings and not only through sense perceptions. This is a part of me that can be described as my radical empirical part in comparison with my classical empirical part, a distinction discussed in the preface. When I'm a radical empiricist, attending to the whole of an experience including the feeling I have, it sometimes seems that, when things begin to come together in unpredictable ways, there is something guiding me. I feel that there may be some kind of spiritual presence watching over me, perhaps guiding my life.

Can this be understood as the presence, the spirit of God? Arthur Peacocke, who was a distinguished biochemist and Anglican priest, and a leader in the science and religion field for several decades before he died in 2006, has developed a form of Christian naturalism that is fully scientific. Things come about due to natural causes. He also holds a theology that stresses the immanence or ever-presence of God. God is in and through the entire universe, and the universe is contained within God, so that God—a personal God—exerts what Peacocke calls "pattern forming influences" to shape events in the world and our lives. When I'm a radical empiricist, I can understand events like my calling to the ministry to be the result of all the various factors coming together under the "pattern forming influence of God."[8]

However, might such an influence also be understood as due to some other kind of spiritual presence? In Florida there is a community, in the tradition of American Spiritualist religion, called Cassadaga. In Cassadaga, there are mediums, mystics, metaphysicians, and others in the American Spiritualist tradition.[9] Their understanding of spiritual presences that shape our lives can include not only God, but also other spiritual realities such as angels, guides, and ancestors. I have found this understanding also in much traditional religion. In other words, what I feel might be guiding me could be one of many kinds of spiritual realities.[10]

The practical result of this part of my thinking, of thinking intuitively or feelingly, is that maybe I'm part of a wider invisible world, some aspects of which are supportive of my life. That wider world may contain realities that I don't understand but experience as friendly and helpful, maybe also realities that are antagonistic and harmful. With this viewpoint, practically I begin to "look" for—sense feelingly—signs of helping presences in the events of my life.

So I appreciate these different parts of me—the naturalistic, rational, classical empirical part; the intuitive, feeling, radical empirical part; and the practical part. They are available to help me understand my experience and to offer practical guidance for living. Yet, regardless of which way I understand how that moment in the outdoor chapel at Camp Onaway came about—maybe it doesn't matter how I understand its origin—it remains for me a thin place that opened up my heart, my self, to new possibilities for my life. It was a liminal moment in which I crossed a threshold and received a new identity, that of minister, an identity that has remained with me in my teaching, writing, and working in various organizations. Regardless of how it happened, it remains for me one of my most significant moments of spiritual transformation.

7

Events of Grace

Reading: Dancing with God

In their book, *Christianity: An Introduction*, Denise and John Carmody suggest that people can live more effectively when they stop trying to control their actions and learn to dance with God.[1]

There is a tantalizing dictum from Christian tradition that puts the covenantal relationship between creator and creatures in the form of a practical maxim. "Act as though everything depended on God and pray as though everything depended on yourself." This maxim is so contrary to most Americans' expectations that frequently they invert it. Surely action, they reason, is our human affair, and prayer is where God comes in. But deeper Christian instinct confounds many other aspects of contemporary Western culture. To the Christian, the priority in all that we observe or do belongs to God the creator, the conserver, the concurer. She is the first cause and the final cause comprehensively.

When people really believe this, Christians assert, their action or work or doing straightens out. Like runners who have learned about stretching, they move easily, with fewer tightnesses and cramps. Like people who have appropriated a trust walk, making it something adult, they let themselves go, expecting that God will catch them when they fall. The results are often impressive. In contrast to the "Type A" behavior of the stereotypic American executive, tightjawed and hell-bent for a coronary, those who feel God's presence keep their work in perspective, taking cues from the subtle initiatives that a given situation offers. Because they are not pushing, they can receive such initiatives, take in the delicate signs that nature or other people give of how things are flowing. Because their egos are not blocking their horizon, they can move their bodies and minds dexterously. So they resemble a realized Zen master, who has no self and can follow Buddha-nature's flow. So they conjure up T. S. Eliot, who set the still point of union with God in the context of a reality that was a dance. "Dance with me," the Christian God says. "Follow my lead, my music of the spheres."

Reflection: Events of Grace

In the last chapter, I suggested some alternative ways of looking at how spiritual transformations occur. One way is to think in naturalistic terms that spiritual transformations arise through serendipitous creativity. Another is to think that they are the result of the activity of a personal presence or presences.

These two alternatives reflect, in my judgment, one of the underlying issues in modern culture regarding how things happen. Those who hold to older human traditions often think that things happen because of the work of invisible personal presences—a variety of presences or a single personal God. One implication of this way of thinking is that things happen as the result of intentions. Just as we humans do things because of our intentions, so events in the natural world are thought to occur as the result of the intentions of God or some other kind of invisible personal realities.

An alternative way of thinking, represented by modern science, is that things happen as the result of complex interactions within the natural world. These interactions do not involve personal presences or intentions. They are the result of nonpersonal, nonintentional forces and processes. Intentionality occurs only when creatures with developed brains, such as humans, are involved.

Much time has been spent in contemporary science and religion discussions about these two ways of understanding how things happen. Many pages of rhetoric and argument have been generated by some of the best scientific, philosophical, and theological minds in the world. One can conclude from all this work that it is very difficult, if not impossible, to resolve intellectually these alternative ways of thinking about how things happen.

This has led me to wonder if it might be helpful simply to focus on the events that happen as we experience them—to focus on our experiences of transformative events in our lives to see how they lead to new self-understandings, new ways of living, and new relationships. It is for this reason that, at the end of the last chapter, I suggested that what was most important to me is not how my calling to ministry happened but the significance of the event, itself, for my life.

When I focus on the events themselves, I find it helpful to call them "events of grace," in order to distinguish them from other kinds of events that occur in our lives. I first developed the idea of an *event of grace* when I was in graduate school in 1966 at Columbia University and Union Theological Seminary in New York City. At that time, I became acquainted with a woman about my age who had many problems. She came from a broken home and was almost homeless. However, she was a devout Roman Catholic, and in spite of all her problems she would sometimes say, "Grace happened to me today!" This phrase startled me. What a peculiar expression, "Grace happened to me." When I listened to what she was describing, I concluded that she was describing an event. It was an event in which something good happened to her, beyond her control.

I took this idea and wrote a paper for one of my professors in which I defined "God" not as a being, not as a person, but as an event—the "grace type event." I suggested in the paper that an event of grace occurs when things beyond our control come together in such a way that they bring about good. My professor liked the paper. On the back of it he wrote, "Excellent. Now the only thing you have to do is define the word *good*."

I think he wrote this because things can come together in ways beyond our control so that the results are bad for us. An automobile accident can injure or take a life. The actions of many people can come together unexpectedly to damage an ecosystem and endanger species. Internationally things can come together in such as way as to bring about a war. So what do events of grace do when they bring about good? How do we know what is good?

To define the word "good," I use an idea from the philosopher of religion Henry Nelson Wieman. In the most general sense, "good" means "relations of mutual support." For example, the notion of *relations of mutual support* is one way to talk about truth: a particular idea is true if it can be related to other ideas and to experiences in mutually supportive ways, so that the idea helps us understand how our experiences come about, and the experiences confirm the idea. *Relations of mutual support* is also a way to talk about beauty. A work of art is a unified and limited whole in which the parts are related to one another and to the whole in mutually vivifying ways.[2] *Relations of mutual support* is a way to talk about a caring community. When people come together in such a way that they are able to show concern and give assistance to one another, so that the members of the community are supported in their living, some good is happening. So an event of grace occurs when things come together in ways beyond our control and give rise to new relations of mutual support such as new truth, new beauty, and new caring in communities.

Events of grace, opening up new possibilities for good, occur all the time. However, they can be facilitated or hindered by the attitudes we take toward what is going on around us. In chapter 3, I followed the thinking of Lewis Sherrill in interpreting events of passage as involving challenges from God. In chapter 4, I introduced the idea of *thin places*. And in the last chapter, I suggested that such events can be seen as serendipitous creativity. Now I want to suggest that events of grace may become more prevalent in our lives if we listen to what is happening around us. You may think that "listening" is a strange metaphor in this context. But it captures what I often find demanded of me. It is not listening to words or other kinds of sounds, but a kind of silent listening, listening mindfully in the present moment, so that one is tuned in to the way things are going in our interactions internally and with one another, and to the way "nature is flowing," as Carmody and Carmody suggest.[3] In addition to listening in this sense, we also have to be open to being led by the events that are happening. This means a willingness to let go of what we have and to be open to new possibilities, to dance with God, following God's leading. Listening and a willingness to be led help to facilitate events of grace—events that increase relations of mutual support and that sometimes transform us.

Let me illustrate what I mean with two examples of events that challenged me to become involved in activities in which I am not normally involved, challenged me to grow in my relationships with others, and transformed my sense of who I am. As I relate them, I hope you will be reminded of times in your own life in which you experienced events of grace.

In April of 2006, my wife Marj and I visited our granddaughter Jana, who was in her first year at the University of Mary Washington in Fredericksburg, Virginia. The university campus was lovely, and it was a beautiful spring weekend with cherry trees and other flowers blooming. We enjoyed two of Jana's classes. We had meals and meaningful conversations with her and four of her friends—the kinds of conversations that make an older generation hopeful about the future. We attended a beautiful concert put on by high school and university choirs. And, on Sunday morning we drove to Arlington, Virginia, to attend worship at an Episcopal church. We went because Jana's women's choir was providing some of the music for worship.

The church was an English-style building—a comfortable house of worship. We sat in the third pew, right behind our granddaughter and her choirmates in a sanctuary that was almost full. The service was conducted by three priests—two of them women. Some of the liturgy was beautifully sung. But, as a Unitarian Universalist and a scientifically-oriented naturalistic theist, I was turned off by the theology of the hymns and the ideas in much of the liturgy. However, the sermon by one of the woman priests, emphasizing love and service, was quite moving. And when our granddaughter and her choirmates sang their first anthem, the crisp pure sound of their harmonious voices was heavenly. From that point on, I experienced a change, a feeling of warmth and love, permeating the atmosphere.

This feeling reminded me of one that I felt years earlier at an ecumenical science and religion meeting, where I was the sole Unitarian Universalist.[4] All the others were from various Christian churches. As the outsider, I was welcomed enthusiastically by open-hearted people. At the end of two days of fruitful discussions, I attended the closing worship service, the Eucharist conducted by the Episcopal clergy. Because I felt that I was in a community of love, I joined my companions in taking communion with them in the presence of love—the presence of Christ.

In Arlington, that same feeling of love was present as the priests and congregation began the celebration of the Eucharist. One of the priests gave a heartfelt invitation to all present to celebrate. Sitting next to Marj, with whom I do not usually attend church because she is a minister of the United Church of Christ and I am a member of a Unitarian Universalist congregation, I realized that this was a rare opportunity to share in a significant religious ritual. I whispered to her, "Let's go up." And we did. To kneel at the communion rail to receive the body and blood of Christ. Jana and a friend from the choir also came to the rail. And so the three of us, none of whom are Episcopalians, celebrated communion together. In that celebration, we grew closer together in love.

I've found that events of grace not only bring about new good in settings of worship and personal relations. Sometimes they lead to a transformation of our identities as we become involved in the wider society. Religion is not only about nurturing our inner life; it sometimes spurs us into social action for justice and peace.

As an academic philosopher of religion, I have spent most of my life trying to understand and appreciate the differences among people regarding their most fundamental, heartfelt convictions. Therefore, I have often found it difficult to take a firm stand on highly charged religious, social, and political issues. However, in 2003 that changed. As I followed the lead of the way things were going in my life, I found myself in what I consider to be a most remarkable event of grace—one that transformed my identity from an intellectual academic to that of activist war protestor. This happened as the United States government was debating whether to go to war in Iraq.

Looking back on it, this event of grace began over thirty-five years ago when I was in graduate school in New York City. I became good friends with Bob and Alice Evans, who lived across the hall in the married students' apartments at Union Seminary. After Bob and I received our degrees, we went our own ways to teach at different schools. But when I moved to Connecticut a few years ago, I discovered that Bob and Alice lived in the neighboring town and that they were good friends with my new wife Marj. So we renewed our graduate-school friendship.

Bob and Alice are the founders and codirectors of an organization called "Plowshares." Plowshares gets it name from the Hebrew Bible vision of world peace: "they shall beat their swords into plowshares, and their spears into pruning hooks."[5] The weapons of war shall become peaceful instruments for growing and harvesting food. Bob and Alice spend about two-thirds of their time each year traveling the world, conducting training sessions in conflict transformation for religious and political leaders. In 2002, their organization, Plowshares, was nominated for the Nobel Peace Prize by two members of the South African parliament for training religious and community leaders in mediation, negotiation, and peace building. The nomination was endorsed by leaders in China and Indonesia and by some members of the United States Congress.

In late December 2002, as director of Plowshares, Bob was invited to go to Iraq with a delegation sponsored by the National Council of Churches. The purposes were to make a humanitarian inspection to see what living conditions were like, especially for women and children, and to seek alternatives to the proposed U.S. invasion. In mid-January 2003, Marj and I went to hear Bob, an ordained Presbyterian minister, preach at the First Presbyterian Church in Hartford. From him I learned the plight of the civilian population. I was surprised to learn that this plight was the result of United Nations sanctions, which were instituted after the 1991 Gulf War. The sanctions made it impossible for Iraqi civilians to get enough food and good drinking water. As a result, 500,000 children under five died from 1992 to 2002. And some estimate that 60 percent of those who survive are malnourished. When Bob was asked to guess the age of a group of Iraqi children, he said they looked to be nine or ten. He was told that they were fifteen and sixteen. Malnutrition had stunted their growth. When I heard this, something happened inside of me. I felt that I really cared about what happened to these children.

As my heart opened up to these children, I had reached a threshold. I had been moving toward this liminal experience for the past couple of weeks as a result of the activity of other people. A couple of weeks earlier, I had heard the minister at my own church invite people to fill shoe boxes with soap, toothpaste, toothbrushes, shampoo, combs, and hairbrushes to send to the people of Iraq. They would be used in a demonstration at the main post office of Hartford. The postal service had a regulation that no package weighing more than twelve ounces could be sent to Iraq. A shoe box of toiletries weighs more than twelve ounces. My own church was just one of many religious communities who were involved. Marj and many of her clergy friends were also joining the demonstration. The goal of the demonstration was to try to mail the boxes and be refused. The event was covered by the media.

But it was Bob's sermon—especially the part about the children—that began to take me over the threshold. So on Wednesday, January 15, 2003, the birthday of Martin Luther King Jr., I joined sixty others in twenty degree weather outside the main post office of Hartford for a half-hour ceremony and for the attempt to mail the boxes.

The ceremony included remarks by a Catholic priest who was the chaplain of the Connecticut State Legislature, the president of Hartford Seminary, a rabbi, a Muslim imam, and some Protestant ministers. They spoke in honor of King and his work for justice and peace. We sang Negro spirituals. During the ceremony, a group of eight went into the post office and returned with their packages. The ceremony closed with a litany led by the Unitarian Universalist minister and with our singing "We Shall Overcome."

I had been very apprehensive about getting involved in this demonstration. It was just not who I was—the careful, thoughtful academic considering all sides of a question. Yet, as events proceeded from the Sunday service where Bob spoke through the next couple of days, I began to let go, to let myself be led by whatever might happen. So I found myself at the post office demonstration.

At first, my role there was as one of the crowd. However, things were happening that, for me, were much more significant. Before the ceremony, I was asked to assist in overseeing the parking. In front of the post office was a busy four-lane highway. Those coming to the demonstration had to be told to park on side streets or in the parking lot of the Red Roof Inn a block away.

Our people gathered about 150 feet from the main road where there was a pickup truck with our boxes to be mailed and a speaker's stand. I and another man were at the highway. The other man knew many of the people, and he guided them to the appropriate parking places. I just stood there. At one point he said, "I think it would help if we had a sign" to identify the demonstration. I looked back at the group and there were large signs with blue background and white lettering—"No War on Iraq." Now, having already let go of the academic part of myself and being quite open to do whatever I was being led to do, I thought to myself: "He's busy with the parking; I guess I'll get the sign." I got the sign and came back. He was still busy telling people where to park as they drove up. And so, moving into what now seemed a natural next step, I said to myself, "I guess I should hold up the sign." So there I stood, by myself, on this busy Hartford street. Cars went past. People looked at me and my sign, saying "No War on Iraq." That is how I underwent a change in self-identity. That is how I became a war protestor.

I share this event not because I am trying to persuade you to stand with me against the war. Many of you may disagree with me. Making a decision whether or not to support our government policies regarding Iraq is a difficult decision that each of us must make for ourselves. And we must care for and about people who disagree with us.

The reason why I share this story is because I think it tells us something about events of grace. Events of grace occur when things happen beyond our control that help us grow in a good way. They are facilitated when we listen to what is going on around us and are open to being led and transformed by the circumstances in which we find ourselves. When we listen and are open, things can come together in unexpected ways to bring about new good such as an increase in loving relationships within a family. And events of grace may also draw us into becoming more actively involved in doing good for others—for the homeless, for the abused, for mistreated animals, for the environment, and for those suffering the ravages of war.

8

Calamitous Convergences

Reading: Struggle

In her book, *Scared by Struggle, Transformed by Hope*, Joan Chittister says that suffering and struggle affect not only what we will do but the kind of person we will be.[1]

> No one comes out of struggle, out of suffering, the same kind of person they were when they went in. It's possible, of course, to come out worse than we were when we went into the throes of pain. Struggle can turn to sour in us, of course. But it is equally possible, if we choose to reflect on it, to come out stronger and wiser than we were when it began. What is not possible, however, is to stay the same.
>
> Struggle is the great crossover moment of life. It never leaves us neutral. It demands that we make a choice: either we dig down deep into the wellspring that is our innermost selves and go on beyond where we were, despite where we were, or we simply give up, stop in our tracks rooted to the spot, up to our ankles in bitterness and

despair, satisfied to be less than all our personal gifts indicate that we are being called to be.

My mother could have given me away to the sister of hers who wanted to raise me. She had every opportunity to do so, after all. And it was certainly the smarter thing to do. She would have been more marriageable had she done it. She could have started all over again without me. After all, she was young and pretty and I was too little to know the difference. Instead, she decided that we would start all over again together. And in her transformation, she transformed me as well. I learned by watching her something I could never have learned simply by hearing about it: I learned that struggle tempers the steel of the soul. It straightens the backbone and purifies the heart. It makes demands on us that change us forever and makes us new. It shows us who we are. Then we make choices, maybe for the first time in life, that determine not only what we'll do in life but what kind of person we'll be for the rest of it.

Reflection: Calamitous Convergences

In the two previous chapters, I've used different metaphors to talk about the kind of transformation that brings new good for us. *Events of grace* are interactions that bring about new relations of mutual support. God as "pattern forming influence" leads to new forms of existence and to deeper and more loving human relationships.[2]

"Serendipitous creativity" also points to the same beneficial activity in the universe, life, human society, and individual living.[3] However, for some, including myself, there seems to be a dark side of God, a way in which events come together so that disaster is the result. I call such events *calamitous convergences*, a counterpoint to serendipitous creativity and events of grace.

In May 2005, I read the novel *The Horse Whisperer*.[4] The opening pages describe how natural events and human decisions can come together in ways that lead to unforeseeable consequences. There's the first snowfall of the season, somewhere in upstate New York, making everything beautiful. A truck driver from Atlanta is delayed overnight by the police. He's been driving for too many hours. He also forgets the chains to his truck and so decides to take a different, safer route to deliver two large generators to a mill. The mill people have given him directions, assuming he will come from a way that is different from the new route he has chosen.

Two girls, ages fourteen and thirteen, Judith and Grace, are on an early morning horseback ride. Because the day is so beautiful, they decide to take a longer route that they don't usually take. Unknown to the girls who are on unfamiliar territory, a culvert has been leaking water, creating a sheet of ice on a hillside leading from the old road to the mill, up to a railroad grade. The ice is covered by the first snow of the year.

As the girls try to ride up the embankment, they begin to hear the noise of a truck coming down the old road, the wrong entrance to the mill. The lead horse slips going up the icy embankment, falls back down on the second horse, pushing both into the path of the oncoming truck. The driver downshifts but can't stop soon enough. He applies the breaks, first cautiously to avoid jackknifing, but then all the way in a final desperate effort. The wheels lock, the truck jackknifes, and Judith and her horse Gulliver are crushed as the trailer swings around and collides with the cab. Grace is injured and will have one leg amputated. Her horse, Pilgrim, survives but is physically and psychologically maimed.

That's the first twenty pages. The rest of the book is how Pilgrim, Grace, her mother Annie, her father, and Tom Booker (the horse whisperer) respond to this tragic event.

When I first read this, I thought to myself, "serendipitous calamity." But this doesn't quite make sense, because *serendipity* means something good happening beyond our control. I talked about this at some length with Marj. She suggested that we call such an event a "calamitous convergence." All of us have experienced calamitous convergences—accidents, infectious disease organisms, body cells becoming malignant and dividing out of control—all kinds of calamitous convergences.

Such convergences don't just change our lives and how we live. Following Joan Chittister, they actually change who we are. They force us to become a new kind of person. The question is, What kind of person will we be? William May, in *The Patient's Ordeal*, also focuses on this question.[5] He suggests that health calamities change our identities. As I said in chapter 1, identity change is one of three ways in which a transformation is spiritual. Two others are becoming open to new possibilities for good and living more fully in our sacred center.

Focusing on identity, May suggests that health crises can challenge our identities in three ways. The first is in relation to our bodies. When we are healthy, we effectively interact with the world through our bodies. They are the means by which we experience our world, the way in which we act on the world in return, and the medium by which we disclose ourselves to the wider world. However, when illness occurs, we may no longer sense things as effectively. We may also be impaired in our actions. And our bodies may disclose us to others as debilitated rather than healthy. A fourteen-year-old girl like Grace, with an amputated leg, appears different to others than a healthy teenager. We are no longer the same; who we are has significantly changed.

A second aspect of our identity involves our relationships with others. As we grow, our identity includes the roles we acquire in our relationships with others in our families, vocations, professions, and organizations. A health catastrophe can transform our relationships with others to that of cancer victim, paraplegic, or AIDS patient—generally to someone whose identity becomes that of a dependent person.[6]

A third way in which illness challenges who we are concerns how we identify with the sacred, what May calls the "transcendent." For May, the transcendent is what ultimately matters to us, our ultimate concern. He says that "most people connect with the transcendent or express their 'ultimate concern' chiefly through rituals." These may include the rituals of organized religion, but they also include "a whole range of repeated actions that conform to and represent the foundational events and the patterns of meaning in people's lives." They include how we respond to challenges, eat, clean ourselves, greet one another, and shut down the day. These repeated actions signal the way we connect with the ultimate.[7] When trauma or disease force an alteration in our fundamental rhythms of life, an alternation in how we experience and act with our body, and an alteration in our relationships with others, a person may never become physically whole or healthy in the same way again. He or she may never be the same person again.

Thus, I think that when calamitous convergences change who we are, we are experiencing a form a form of spiritual transformation—a negative spiritual transformation. When such change occurs, it is not enough to ask, what can we do? Because it affects who we are and can affect who we are for the rest of our lives, calamitous convergences lead us to ask the question implied by Joan Chittister, "What kind of person will I be?"

There are long traditions in cultures that address this question. Two prominent ones are rooted in the thinking of the Greek philosopher Aristotle and in Confucian thought in ancient China. Both focus on how we can develop excellences of character—virtues—that enable us to live well even in the face of adversity. Some virtues we have mentioned earlier in this book, for example, open heartedness, compassion, faith, and love. In their essay "Mindful Virtue, Mindful Reverence" in *Zygon: Journal of Religion and Science*, Ursula Goodenough and Paul Woodruff discuss four virtues—courage, humaneness, fair-mindedness, and reverence.[8] Courage is the capacity to balance confidence and fear. Humaneness is the capacity to see with appropriate feeling how other people's situations are like our own. Some call this *empathy*, others call it *compassion*. Fair-mindedness is the capacity to recognize what is just and to be angry at what is unjust. And reverence is the capacity for awe and respect that "allows us to balance our personal ambitions with the sense that we are in a context that is vastly larger and more important than our selves."[9]

As I read the rest of *The Horse Whisperer,* what I found most interesting was how some of these qualities of character seemed to help people respond to the calamity. The mother, Annie Graves, was not a particularly likeable character. She was a hard-driving businesswoman, a manager who fired people. She also was a perfectionist who just would not take "no" for an answer. While her perfectionism sometimes had negative consequences, in the course of the novel this "not taking no" turns out to be a virtue—the virtue of persistence, coupled with the virtue of courage. With these, she is able to open up a window—a window of possibility for the healing of her daughter and her daughter's horse.

Tom Booker, the horse whisperer, seemed to have a sense of reverence, a sense of being a part of a larger scheme of things that helps create the remarkable ending for the novel. And he had another human capacity that Goodenough and Woodruff call *mindfulness*. Tom works with horses and with people in a Buddhist-like way, always fully in the present moment, able to sense an animal's feeling states. I wonder whether he might be a kind of Buddhist equine psychotherapist.

Goodenough and Woodruff describe mindfulness as "knowledge or wisdom that pulls the whole mind and heart of the knower toward a connection with the way things are in all their exciting particularity."[10] I remember the first person whom I experienced as being in a state of mindfulness. It was some years ago at a conference, "Prayer and Spirituality," at Rollins College. One of the key people at that conference was a Zen Buddhist nun. Her name was Geshin. We were in the lounge in the building that housed our department, about forty people sitting around the room. We were having a vigorous intellectual go at prayer and spirituality, with all their implications. In the midst of our intense discussion, Geshin raised her hand and said, "Do you hear the bird outside, singing?" I realized at that point that she had a kind of awareness of what was going on that included not only what we were talking about, but also the whole environment around us. She was connected "with the way things are in all their exciting particularity."

Goodenough and Woodruff go on to suggest that mindfulness is not so much a virtue as something that underlies the virtues. When we are mindful— when we are in a calm state of centeredness—we become aware of all things in our situation, our capacities for responding, and our limitations that lead us to call for help from others. When we are mindful, we can draw on courage to balance confidence and fear; we can see how other people's situations are like our own; we can discern what is fair and not fair; and we can sense that we are part of a larger reality as it is working in our lives, calling us, leading us.

How do we come to have these virtues and mindfulness? I wonder if they may be partly rooted in our biology as predispositions or capacities. Just as we have biological predispositions for fear and anger, we might also have predispositions for courage, naturally selected as a capacity that enabled our ancestors to face danger in seeking food and defending against predators. Likewise, humaneness and fair-mindedness probably helped the development of social cooperation in small-scale societies. And reverence, the capacity to see ourselves as a part of a larger scheme of things, might allow people to be led into new ways of living and even to sacrifice themselves for the greater good.

The same biological rootedness may be true for mindfulness. Jean Kristeller and others have suggested that we've evolved to have attentive capacities, so that when something suddenly happens, we immediately focus on it—a kind of startle response.[11] I wonder whether we also have some evolved capacity to tune ourselves to all things that are going on around us in all their particularity. I wonder whether being able to be fully in the present moment may have helped our ancestors in the forests and savannahs in their search for food and avoidance of danger.

Please notice that I'm suggesting that these might be only partly biological. I also think that these capacities need to be cultivated. The cultural environments of family, school, religious communities, and the wider society make a difference in the development of these capacities. So I want to say that the virtues—the qualities of character that help us respond to calamitous convergences—are both biologically supported and also can be cultivated through moral and religious education in a society. Likewise, mindfulness, the state of being in *self* or being in our sacred center, also can be cultivated through a variety of religious practices that help us to focus fully in the present moment on what is happening to us and on how we can respond.

Ironically, sometimes even a calamitous convergence can help cultivate the capacity of mindfulness and call forth whatever virtues we might have developed. When we are confronted with disaster or disease, we might become transformed into a state of simply living day to day, moment by moment, with full attention to what is happening within and around us.

Circumstances were such in my own experience. This happened when my first wife Carol and I were confronted with her incurable cancer. As we moved through this calamitous convergence, as my wife's life was fading and our own physical relationship was coming to an end, we were pressed by the disease of cancer to focus on the present—on the day-to-day, hour-to-hour, moment-to-moment periods of our existence. Whether it was getting up in the morning, changing bandages in the middle of the night, eating, moving about the house, responding to breakthrough pain, going to church, or having friends over to visit, we were led by our disease to be in the present. In present moments, we were called to be open to whatever new good might come our way, no matter how small. And new good did come: new ideas from books we read aloud together, the expertise of our compassionate oncologist who helped us control pain while maintaining intellectual clearheadedness, loving care from visiting nurses and health-care aids, the completion of Carol's last watercolor painting by a newfound friend, food from a neighbor we hardly knew, and the sight of an eagle swooping down from the sky to catch fish near the shore of our lake.

Looking back on this experience, I realize that, in its own way, the disease facilitated the same thing that various forms of meditation, prayer, or psychotherapy may accomplish—giving up attachments to the things of this world and experiencing fully, in the present, whatever life has to offer. A calamitous convergence transformed us into the rhythms of the sacred and became an event of grace.[12] Of course, the disastrous event of cancer could also have destroyed our spirits. Somehow, over the years we had acquired some qualities of character with which we could confront suffering with some degree of mindfulness, courage, and humaneness. We also were blessed with supportive family and friends. And so in the midst of calamity we were able to be open to new possibilities for grace, for serendipitous creativity, for the coming together of new good out of the further interactions of various people, communities, and the wider environment.

Something like this also is illustrated by further developments in *The Horse Whisperer*. But I'm not going to describe how that happens. I don't want to spoil the story for those who haven't read this novel. Instead, I'll close this chapter with an example of how calamitous convergence seems to have become transformed into serendipitous creativity in the real-life story of Alexandra Scott. In August 2004, Alexandra Scott died.[13] She was eight years old and lived the last seven years of her life fighting cancer, a particularly treacherous form of pediatric cancer, neuroblastoma. At age four-and-a-half, Alex decided to set up a lemonade stand in the front yard of her West Hartford, Connecticut, home, in order to raise some money to help find a cure for kids with cancer. Some say it was a visible symbol of Alex's attitude: "If life gives you lemons, make lemonade."

Her idea caught on. Others began to open stands in Alex's name. When she moved from West Hartford to Wynnwood, Pennsylvania, the community there also got involved. Today one can find Alex's lemonade stands across the country from Connecticut to Arizona, from Florida to Wisconsin. Even after her death, Alex keeps selling lemonade. Her parents and others are carrying on in her name, carrying on her mission. To see what's happening I suggest you visit the Web site http://www.alexslemonade.org. It's an inspiring site. By June 2007, over twelve million dollars had been raised for research on pediatric cancer.

The lesson I learn from Alex's story is this: when we experience calamitous convergence, we don't have to succumb to the calamity as the end. New good can follow calamity if we have mindfulness, if we have virtues that open us up to being able to discern and realize new possibilities for good emerging in the midst of death, disease, and despair. Moving from calamitous convergence to serendipitous creativity is another kind of spiritual transformation. Through suffering, we can come to experience the grace of God.

9

Dying

Reading: "Out of the Stars"

In this responsive reading from the Unitarian
Universalist hymnal, Robert Weston gives a
poetic rendition of what some scientists are calling the "epic of evolution."[1]

> Out of the stars in their flight,
>   out of the dust of eternity,
>   here have we come,
> Stardust and sunlight,
>   mingling through time and through space.
> Out of the stars have we come,
>   up from time;
> Time out of time before time
>   in the vastness of space,
>   earth spun to orbit the sun,
> Earth with the thunder of mountains newborn,
>   the boiling of seas.
> Earth warmed by the sun, lit by sunlight:
> This is our home;
>   out of the stars have we come.

Mystery hidden in mystery,
    back through all time;
Mystery rising from rocks
    in the storm and the sea.
Out of the stars, rising from rocks and the sea,
    kindled by sunlight on earth arose life.
Ponder this thing in your heart;
    ponder with awe:
Out of the sea to the land,
    out of the shallows came ferns.
Out of the sea to the land,
    up from darkness to light,
Rising to walk and to fly,
    out of the sea trembled life.
Ponder this thing in your heart,
    life up from sea;
Eyes to behold, throats to sing,
    mates to love.
Life from the sea, warmed by sun,
    washed by rain,
Life from within, giving birth, rose to love.
This is the wonder of time;
    this is the marvel of space;
Out of the stars swung the earth;
    life upon earth rose to love.
This is the marvel of life,
    rising to see and to know;
Out of your heart, cry wonder:
    sing that we live.

Reflection: Dying

Just after Christmas 2004, I received a phone call that I expected but didn't want to get. It was my cousin, saying that my wife Marj and I should come as quickly as we could. My mother had taken a turn for the worse, and they didn't know how long she would live.

On the flight to Wisconsin from Hartford, Connecticut, I remembered this woman—my stepmother who for almost fifty years had been mother to me. On December 18, she had celebrated her ninety-eighth birthday. She was relatively healthy for her age, although very frail. She said she was beyond old. The next day she rode fifty miles with my cousins to a family celebration of her birthday and Christmas. The following Tuesday, the Tuesday before Christmas, Mom was playing bingo in the retirement center and nursing home where she lived. She slumped over in her chair. A stroke disabled the left side of her body.

At that time, our youngest granddaughter was five months old. When I arrived, the first thing I did was to show my mother a picture of her newest great-granddaughter. Mom died on the second day in January, 2005.

The death of my mother and the birth of our granddaughter are biological transformations— death and birth. What makes them spiritual transformations?

Often people think about these transformations in terms of what happens to the person who is born or dies. This raises questions about the nature of the person. Is there a spirit or soul that enters or leaves the body? Does life continue after death? If so, how? There are a variety of answers to these questions from the world's religions. Hindus claim that a person's soul or essence is reincarnated. Each person exists both before and after life as we now know it. I once heard a Hindu say, "I've lived a million lifetimes." Buddhists also believe in reincarnation but not in a substantial soul. Instead, something like one's character is passed on, analogous to a flame of one candle lighting the flame of another. Often Christians and Muslims, influenced by the dualistic thinking of Greek philosophy that separates body and soul, believe that a person's soul separates from the body at death and goes to heaven or hell (or purgatory). Other Christians, drawing on biblical Jewish thought, affirm the unity of one's soul and body. They believe in a resurrection in a new bodily form—a spiritual body. Some Jews also believe this, while other Jews, as well as many others, focus on how a person lives on in the memories of those still alive and in the influences one has exerted on others and the rest of the world. So, while those in a particular religious tradition may firmly believe that their understanding of life after death is the true one, there is no uniform worldwide set of beliefs about whether and how we may preexist this life or continue to exist after it.

In the preface, I suggested that my own thinking is grounded in experience. This leads me to
wonder if there is any kind of experience that may
help us understand what happens when we die.
One possibility is the near-death experiences of
people who appear, even medically, to have died
but who revive, even to good health. Bruce Greyson, editor of the *Journal of Near-Death Studies*,
says that some studies suggest that perhaps as
many as 5 percent of the United State's population have had such experiences (although he says
this may be high).[2] While a small percentage of
the population may not seem like much, we must
keep in mind that the circumstances under which
such experiences can occur and be documented
are quite rare.

Greyson notes that for individuals whose
closeness to death can be corroborated by medical
records, the more common experiences are those
of a bright light, increased cognitive functioning,
and positive emotions. A common emotion is the
experience of unconditional love. Even though
there is no correlation as to whether and how a
person was religious before the experience and
even though theologians respond differently as to
what such experiences mean for their own faiths,
one interesting finding has to do with the results of
such experiences. In the opening summary of his
article "Near-Death Experiences and Spirituality,"
Greyson writes that near death experiences "lead
to a shift from ego-centeredness to other centeredness, a disposition to love unconditionally,

heightened empathy, decreased interest in status symbols and material possessions, reduced fear of death, and deepened spiritual consciousness."[3]

In reviewing Greyson's article, I'm struck by how near-death experiences, themselves, are transformations of identity, and how well these transformations fit with some of the ideas we've been discussing, such as being in *self* or in our sacred center, moving from closed to open hearts, and moving from fear to being at peace. They also fit with the idea of living in an evolving universe that emerges into a form of life that can experience and act in love. Echoing Robert Weston's poetry in our reading, we can say that we have come out of the stars, and we have come up from life—to love.

While this love is often experienced in near-death experiences and while it flows from these experiences after a person recovers, love is also important for those who are with someone who is dying. For the rest of this chapter, I'll focus on the family, friends, and caregivers who may be with a dying person. This leads to the issue of relationships: how we think of ourselves as related to one another and to our wider world. I'd like to lift up two kinds of relationships that are important in the process of dying. One relationship we can call *meaning.* The other we can call *love.*

One way to understand *meaning* is by relating parts to a whole. A way I do this is to try to understand my living and dying in the context of the history of the universe, which some scientists call the "epic of evolution." Death and birth are a part of this epic. One aspect of the meaning of the epic, of the ongoing creation of the universe that we call evolution, is that death gives rise to new opportunities for existence.

We see this in the death of stars. Stars the mass of our sun go through their life sequences of burning hydrogen and creating helium through nuclear fusion. Then, as they use up their fuel, they begin to collapse and their temperature increases. Helium begins to fuse until it is used up, and, again, the stars collapse under gravity. Other elements begin to burn until there is nothing more that can be fused together. But as a result of this process new elements are created—elements like oxygen, nitrogen, carbon, and even iron. In stars the mass of our sun, elements heavier than iron cannot be created; the temperatures are simply not high enough. However, in giant stars ten times the mass of our sun, for example, the process is more dramatic. In their final collapse, under tremendous gravitational forces, the star implodes, then rebounds, creating temperatures so great that even the most complex of the natural elements are born. These are then flung out into space in a gigantic explosion called a supernova. Eventually the elements coalesce back together under the influence of gravity to form a new generation of stars, some with planetary systems. One of these new star systems with planets is our own solar system, with all of the elements that, on earth, gave rise to life and human beings. If earlier, massive stars had not exploded, had not died in their own way, we would not be here. Out of those stars, in our region of the universe, we have come. Death gives rise to possibilities for life.

I think we can look at human history and see how death gives rise to new possibilities. For example, the Roman Empire was preceded by the empire of Alexander the Great. When Alexander's empire disintegrated after the death of Alexander and the Romans finally defeated the Greeks, people discovered that Greek philosophy, Greek culture, Greek poetry became fused into the Roman political system. The Greek civilization died but gave birth to new possibilities of culture for the Romans. Then, when the Roman Empire collapsed and died, Roman law and other practices became transformed when combined with Christianity in European civilization. We are the inheritors of the deaths of the Greek and Roman civilizations with our law, our philosophy, and much of our culture. Death gives rise to new opportunities for human society and culture.

The same is true of all of us as individuals—true of my mother. As we go through life, we influence one another for better or for worse. Those influences are not only remembered. They also impinge on people's lives below the level of conscious memories. And so as we live and die, we give rise to new possibilities that granddaughters and great-granddaughters will have as a result of our being here. This I think is part of the meaning—

life out of stars, giving rise to humans, and to new generations of humans in societies.

In this picture of birth and death in the history of the universe, evolution gives rise to love between human beings. This is the second kind of relationship I want to talk about—the relationship of love. In my own experience over the years, I have found that when a loved one is dying, new possibilities for love arise even in that dying process.[4] In fact, sometimes all one can do when a loved one is dying is to be with them in love.

As Marj and I stayed with my mother during her final days, I observed a change that took place among those who were with her. At the nursing home where Mom lived, the staff was very concerned about people eating, always calibrating how much they were to have on their plates, their proper diets, and always recording how much had been eaten. Their goal was to make sure the residents got enough nourishment. Their goal was to keep them alive.

After her stroke, however, my mother was no longer able to eat well. I observed that the staff at the home became less and less concerned with making sure she got enough food. Instead, they focused on giving her whatever she could take in. In one particular instance I observed a young woman no longer giving her food, but giving thickened water to keep her mouth moist. As my mother sat with her eyes closed and partly slumped over, this young woman very carefully—

mindfully focused in the present moment—took a spoon, a little spoon partly filled with thickened water, and moved it up to my mother's mouth. When it touched her lips, her mouth opened, the spoon went in, and the liquid went in. After some difficulty my mother swallowed, and the young woman took the spoon away. That was a loving act, a mindfully loving act that this woman was doing for my mother.

There were others who changed my mother's position with the same deliberate, careful, caring activity. There were those who visited her, talked with her, held her hand—family, friends, her minister, church members—in love. And finally, I did one of the most difficult things I've done in my life. I gave her permission to die—with love.

I had learned from counselors and ministers that sometimes when people are in the final stages of their life, they might hang on longer than they really need to. They might suffer more. But if someone close to them gives them permission to let go, to die, it eases the dying process.

The way I did this was to draw on the relationship between my mother and my father. Mom and Dad had been loving companions for over forty-five years. My dad died in 2000 at the age of ninety-four. And, from what my mother had told me, I realized that they had talked about dying. They had talked about who might go first. Actually, the plan was for my mother to go first, so that my mother didn't have to live on alone after my father went. Only it didn't work that way. They even talked about what they would wear at the funeral service. Mom had her dress all picked out. It was a dress that Dad, years before, had asked her to wear so that, if he did go first, he could recognize her more easily when she came into what she called "the great beyond." But one time, when we visited a couple of years ago, she took me aside and said, "I don't think it works like that."

With all this in my mind, I waited for an opportunity when I could be alone with her, at her side. When that opportunity came, I took her hand in my hands, leaned over to her, and gently said, "Mom, I think it's time to be with Dad again." I said this choking back a sob, with tears in my eyes. She couldn't respond, but I noticed a tear forming in the corner of her left eye.

I think that such acts of loving relationship are spiritual acts. And all those who engaged in them during the days and hours of my mother's dying were transformed as they stopped trying to keep a life going, let go, and only loved.

In the same year of my mother's death, at the end of May, a good friend of mine died. Jim was a retired professor of literature, and he and I had gotten to know each other in our church. Because we shared teaching at the college level and other interests in our church, we began to get together for regular lunches. Every Tuesday, when we both were in town, we would go to a restaurant and order French onion soup and decaf coffee. As we ate, we had conversations, sometimes very personal conversations.

I referred to us as the "ROMEOS." Some years ago at a meeting, one of the older men had asked some of us if we knew what the term *romeo* meant. We replied, "No." He said, "Retired old men eating out." I modified that a little bit in thinking about Jim and me, and added an "s"—*romeos*—retired old men eating onion soup. It was our private joke.

In the fall of 2003, Jim, who had already overcome two kinds of cancer, was diagnosed with leukemia, with no really helpful treatment available. His bone marrow was unable to produce blood cells the way it should. As the weeks and months went by, he grew more and more tired. He had blood transfusions, and these would revive him for a few weeks, so he could go out to the theater or to a symphony concert with a friend. But after each transfusion the time between transfusions got shorter and shorter, until he was no longer able to go out for lunch. So he and I visited in his home. As he grew more disabled, friends and family came to help him. Especially helpful were visits from his three children, who took off from their work and families in other parts of the country to come, to visit, and to help.

Jim wasn't afraid of dying. He just didn't want to talk about it very much. Three weeks before his death, I tried to discuss with him my religious outlook about how, in the midst of the worst times, some new good might emerge. He argued with me on that. But, as we continued to talk, we did uncover some examples of small goods that might be possible for him in his final days.

When I returned a week later, he said, "You know, one good thing has happened. I've come to realize how much my children love me." I had the opportunity to tell this to some of his family members a month later when we were planning his memorial service. When I told them about the love Jim had experienced, his son said, "That's what we were trying to do!"

As the Weston reading states: "Out of the stars have we come. . . . / Out of the sea to the land, up from darkness to light, / Rising to walk and to fly, out of the sea trembled life. / Ponder this thing in your heart, life up from sea; / Eyes to behold, throats to sing, mates to love. / Life from the sea, warmed by the sun, washed by the rain, / Life from within, giving birth, rose to love. / This is the wonder of time; this is the marvel of space; / Out of the stars swung the earth; life upon earth rose to love."

And so when life is fading, love can grow, and when loves grows, it has meaning as part of the epic of the evolution of the universe, an epic of transformations that gives birth to the new out of the old that dies. And when love grows between human beings, relationships deepen even in the last moments of life. And those continuing to live are changed in the spiritual transformation of hearts opening up in increasing love.

10

Living Now in Eternity

Reading: Being Responsible for Eternity

The following passage by Max Rudolf Lemberg, a Quaker Christian and a distinguished scientist, expresses the responsibility we have in living our lives. [1]

> I believe that eternity does not begin after my death; it was before I came and will remain when I die. But above all it is during my life here on earth, and this is indeed the only time during which I am responsible for my contribution to it. . . . It is, I believe, untrue that what I have done during my life, however insignificant in itself, will not count from the viewpoint of eternity. What I mean is not that it will be remembered. Nobody remembers the man who split the first flint or lit the first fire. . . . Nobody remembers the first woman who spun or planted seeds. My individual unity may be remembered for a few years and that of the great man, Jesus, for thousands of years. It is not important whether my name or any special deed of mine will be remembered; it will certainly

not be remembered forever. However, what I have done, whatever it was, good or evil, has become eternal in the sense that it has become an indestructible irremovable part and parcel of the tissue of life of humanity. . . . Not only books or discoveries or statements but even passing acts of generosity or lack of it—anything which has influenced other persons, adult or child, belongs to the eternal realm, even a mere loving act, thought, or gesture. That I shall not survive my uniqueness of person may be a serious blow to my self-love, but the contributions of myself and millions of other persons are not in vain.

Reflection: Living Now in Eternity

One of the themes of this book is that we are always living on the edge of time. Each moment of our lives is part of a developmental path that has come into being in the fourteen-billion-year history of the universe. We are in a state of continuous becoming, and, as we grow throughout our lives, we undergo a number of transformations. These transformations are spiritual transformations insofar as who we are—our identity—changes in significant ways: in the ways we experience and act in the word, in the relationships we have with others, and in the basic rhythms of our lives. They also are spiritual transformations inasmuch as we realize new possibilities for good and insofar as we become more and more able to live in a state of calm, curious, creative, and compassionate mindfulness that we can call our *sacred center*. We might say that, in this state, we are living now in eternity.

I can think of two meanings for the word *eternity* that are consistent with the ideas in this book and that are grounded in human experience. The first is that of the great Christian thinker Saint Augustine. For Augustine *eternity* does not mean endless time but the opposite of time.[2] It is the stillness of the present moment in which time stops but in which all things present are experienced in their amazing particularity. For Augustine, it is only God who intimately knows all things at once. However, a limited human being can still become mindful, fully awake to all things in the present moment. The Buddhists call this *enlightenment*; the name *Buddha* means "enlightened or awake." I have called it being in *self* or in our sacred center.

A second meaning of *eternity* refers to a process of divine creating that has been going on for billions of years and will continue for billions of years into the future. It is a process in which we are now living. Even though we may seem infinitesimal in the vast universe, we still have been created through its evolutionary processes to be able to reflect about where we are and to ask about our place in this grand, eternal scheme of things. As we do this, we might also think about our responsibility for that part of this grand scheme that has given rise to human beings and all creatures we know, namely, our earth-sun system. With the energy of the sun, our earth, created out of elements forged in older exploding stars, has given rise to millions of living creatures over millions of years. One creature, the human, is capable of seeing the value of all of this, capable of affirming its goodness. And with this affirmation comes the question: how are we called to enhance good in our world, not only among humans but among all forms of life?

With these two views of eternity, I suggest that we find ourselves in a position of responsibility. It is responsibility for the future. What kinds of new possibilities for existence are we being called to enable. It is the responsibility mentioned by the Jewish scholar Louis Finklestein in chapter 2, responsibility for making the world a holy place.[3] It also is the responsibility of those who recognize with Jesus that the Kingdom of God is within us, in the midst of us. It is the responsibility implied in the question: how are we being led to live in the midst of eternity?

As we live out our own developmental paths, we also are part of wider and longer historical paths of social and cultural becoming. Further, our human social histories are intertwined with the histories of other species and with the rhythms of our planet. I experienced some sense of these multiple paths when I recently attended my fiftieth high-school class reunion in Fond du Lac, Wisconsin. As I was attending the reunion, I reflected not only on the course of my life but also on some of the things my classmates had done. I realized that each of them, like me, has gone through some of the spiritual transformations I have described. Each has undergone changes in their identity, in their relationships, and in the basic rhythms of their lives. Most have experienced death and some new form of life. So I can imagine how we all, in our own particular ways, are particular streams of life, mind, and heart that have arisen on planet Earth.

I then thought about the fact that in this small city, there was another class of students after ours, and another after that, and then still others—both before and after. It was as if each year the city had produced a crop of children and, with its families, schools, churches and synagogues, had cultivated them to adulthood. This metaphor fit with the fact that Wisconsin is a state with much farming. Each year farmers cultivate the earth and produce new crops of corn and cattle. Along with the farm crops are new generations of deer, pheasant, bear, and other wildlife. The earth is producing all kinds of creatures that, like us, grow and live through the cycles of their lives.

Each of these—each human, animal, plant, bird, insect—each creature is a complex system with a long history. If we could know enough, the history of each individual could be traced back to the origin of the universe, to the energy that was transformed into atoms of hydrogen and helium, into more complex atoms in exploding stars, into life forms on planet Earth, and, with humans, into creatures that could reflect back on this whole process. Each individual is a particular stream of energy, matter, and life that flowed out of the original inflation called the big bang. Wow! Each of us is fourteen billion years old—all human beings and all the individuals of other life-forms on the planet.

Reflecting on this, I felt how precious is each individual creature! How wonderful the productive earth that is the mother of us all! How mysterious and amazing the sacred creative process that brought us all into being! And, with this sense of the value of all things and the wonder of all of creation, I felt a sense of responsibility—responsibility for my brief time on earth. I understood what Max Lemberg meant when he said about himself that, "during my life on earth. . . , I am responsible for my contribution to [eternity]."[4]

But then I realized that some of my classmates have not had a full life. And many in our world do not have the opportunities that I have had. They, too, were born on the edge of time as a result of a vast universal history. But their circumstances did not allow them to become what they might have become. Life is not always fair. Some are born to good, long lives, and some are born to lives of struggle and early death. I also felt a sense of injustice thinking about when the more vulnerable are exploited and abused by those in power.

And a part of me felt anger when I thought how human beings continue to exploit the resources of our planet at the expense of other species and of future human generations.

With all this in mind, I begin to wonder about the future. As I do this I think about some ideas that we have explored in this book, especially the ideas of *calling* and *being led*. Recognizing the suffering and injustice in or world, especially as created by humans, I am led to ask, what is our current situation calling us to become as we move on the edge of time into the future?

How we answer this question depends in part on what kind of stories we tell about our world and ourselves. Some suggest that, among other things we can do, we should be the storytellers of the universe. This echoes an insight of the biologist Julian Huxley, namely, that in humans "evolution was at last becoming conscious of itself."[5] Think about that. In humans, the universe has become conscious of itself. This means that one of our purposes of living, as a symbolic species, is to tell the "universe story."[6]

What is our place in this story, especially on our planet Earth? Some who tell the story of the universe regard humans as the apex of evolution—the culmination. They tell and live a story in which humans are the conquerors and rulers of planet Earth. This story of conquest and domination is especially prevalent in our American culture. Perhaps it is our dominant story. Others, including me, want to tell another story. This story understands the history of the universe as a history in which all things are connected in one large natural family, in which all share the energy of the universe, the matter created in stars, and the resources of our planet. This is a story of sharing, of promoting biological and cultural diversity, of respecting different ways of living. It is a story not of conquest, but of citizenship. Aldo Leopold writes about this contrast in his "land ethic," saying that "a land ethic changes the role of *homo sapiens* from conqueror of the land-community to plain member and citizen of it. It implies respect for [our] fellow members, and also respect for the community as such."[7] This is the story of friendship—of being friends with all human beings and with all of creation.

A powerful metaphor that represents these two stories is expressed by a Chinese Taoist philosopher, who suggests two ways of portraying the climbing of Mt. Everest. We might say that Mt. Everest represents the goal of human life. The philosopher says: "When you Westerners climb Mt. Everest, you say 'We have conquered Mt. Everest.' However, we Taoists would say, 'We have befriended Mt. Everest.'"[8]

A small example of the attitudes in these two ways of understanding human purpose occurred at breakfast on our porch this summer. As my wife and I sat down to eat, I noticed that an insect was struggling to free itself from an old spider web at the top of the doorway. The spider was gone and so the web it had created to trap food no longer served that purpose. But the flying insect was caught just the same. Carefully, I took the web down and set it on the ground. With the added traction from being in touch with the earth, the insect was able to free itself. As I returned to breakfast, my wife commented, "Yeah. And we send our young people off to war!"

So we can tell and live stories of conquest or stories of befriending! What kind of story do we want to tell as we live on the edge of time? More important: what kind of story are we being called to *live* as we help create our future and the future of life on our planet?

During the holiday season of 2006, I once again heard a story that I had heard many times before, the Christmas story of the birth of Jesus. During the worship service, our minister told it first as a children's story, and it was then retold in Heinrich Schütz's "The Christmas Story," an oratorio of the birth of Christ.[9]

After the children had gathered around her in the front of our church, the Reverend Barbara Jamestone told about the announcement of the birth of Jesus to Mary. "Behold . . . . a savior of the world." She then asked what it meant to say Jesus was the savior of the world. How did Jesus save the world? The answer she gave the children, and the rest of us, was that God so loved the world that God sent his son. And this son exhibited completely the love of God. That love set up a chain of love from Jesus, first to his disciples and then though succeeding generations, all the way down to the present day. And our job, she told the children, is to "keep the love chain going—to love all people, whoever they are, as Jesus did."

After the children left to go to their religious education classes, our church choir performed Schütz's oratorio. In music and scripture readings, I heard once again the story of Mary and Joseph going to Bethlehem, of the shepherds in the field hearing the announcement of the birth from the angel, and of the wise men following the star and inquiring of Herod where the child might be. Then something happened that led me into a transformation of feelings and understanding. The baritone from the choir strode to the center of the chancel. He was Herod. And because of the way he conducted himself, his posture and his gestures, as he sang the text of Herod speaking to the wise men, I realized that I was witnessing evil. It was the evil of deception as Herod told the wise men to find Jesus and then to come and tell him, so that he might go and "worship" Jesus also. It was the evil of power—of the abuse of power. When the wise men did not return, Herod ordered all the male children of Palestine to be killed, so that the foretold Messiah would not survive.

It was at that point that I realized the mythic conflict present in the story of the birth of Jesus— the conflict between love and power. It was the kind of love that reaches out to all people, to those who are sick and disabled, to those who are poor and oppressed, to those who are the outcasts of society. And it was the kind of power–corrupted, self-serving, abusive–that slays innocent children to stay in power. Chills went through me as I saw Herod before me in the person of our choir's baritone, threatening the evil that was to come. It was especially chilling in contrast to the annunciation to Mary that she would give birth to the savior of the world–the one who would inaugurate the love chain that was to be for all people.

Like the Taoist story of the climbing of Everest– a story of conquest or of befriending–the Christmas story that I heard and saw portrayed, presented to me two ways of living on the edge of time–living by the power that destroys in order to preserve itself, or by the love that enables all people to flourish and fulfill their potential.

This is a choice we have to make. But, also, there is a calling from the science-based account of the history of the universe through all its transformations and its suggestion that each of us has a history that goes back to the beginning, as well as from the biblical story of Jesus and Herod–both together call me, lead me to want to live my life with compassion for the well-being of all things.

Throughout this book, I have been using Victor Turner's model of spiritual transformation. Even though the model suggests that the culmination of spiritual transformation is reached in a liminal or threshold state, a "mountaintop experience," it is significant that the model ends with a return to daily life. One cannot stay on the mountain. The point of undergoing spiritual transformation is not the transformative experience, itself, but the results of that experience as we return to our daily lives. One of my favorite ways of conveying this point is with the famous oxherding pictures of Zen Buddhism. Here I will show, in figure 1, six oxherding pictures from *A Flower Does Not Talk* by Zenkei Shibayama.[10] In their own way, these pictures portray the process of spiritual transformation and its results. And they call us to a form of "playing" in a life of compassion for the well-being of all—to a life that in some versions of these pictures is titled "Entering the City with Bliss-Bestowing Hands."[11]

1. Six Oxherding Pictures

Awakening of Faith

The First Entering

Not Thoroughly
Genuine Yet

True Mind

Both Forgotten

Playing

The first thing I see in the pictures is that they show a movement from unenlightenment or ignorance (the black ox), to enlightenment (the white ox) in picture four. They also show a movement from dualistic thinking with its fears and desires into a state of tranquil unity. Notice the tension in picture one and the tranquility in picture four. This contrast between these two pictures also suggests a process of taming the wild ox of our desires when they run out of control. And they show, in picture five, a breakthrough to a new way of being, called "both forgotten," a state that Buddhists sometimes call "emptiness" or "suchness." This is the state of being in the sacred center that I have called by a variety of names in this book. Without self-protective egoistic desires, this state is like a perfectly polished mirror that accurately reflects all things as they really are.

Finally, the pictures show a return to daily life, but now transformed into a different way of living called *playing*. This playing is living fully in the present and being fully available to others. Shibayama writes: "the 'I' which has once thoroughly cast away both its mind and body and revived from the 'Both Forgotten' is no longer the former I. This body and this life now live anew. In other words, it is the life given by the Great Love of the Buddha. It is the life that is to work as the Buddha's hands and feet. It is, again, the source of creation which will give love and light wherever it goes."[12] This is what it means to live a life of playing with bliss-bestowing hands.

But how might one give love and light to others? How might one live with bliss-bestowing hands? When I taught ethics courses at Rollins College, one of the problems I encountered was the problem of doing good for others. People often want to help others, to work for the benefit of others. But ethicists sometimes point out that we don't always know what will actually be beneficial for others.

More important, when we think we do know, we often end up projecting our own ideas as to what we would like for ourselves onto others. We don't listen to what others really need. When this happens, often those who claim to be doing good become "do gooders," whose *good* actions miss the mark.

I think Buddhism and other religions have a helpful insight here. It is that before we can help others, we have to let go of being attached to our own interests, to let go of our self-protective egos, and become the kind of person who is *playing*. This means taking things as they come, taking others as they come. It means being in *self*, listening to the way things are going, opening our hearts to people in need, being mindful of their needs and mindful of our limitations. Shibayama has an interesting way of putting it. He says it means "assuming whatever shape according to the conditions."[13] Assuming whatever shape according to the conditions? That's playing when you think about it—the playing of young children. Becoming as a little child, Jesus says, one can enter the kingdom of heaven. When one becomes like this, one is living now in eternity.

Shibayama concludes his essay on the six oxherding pictures with the following story that illustrates this idea of assuming whatever shape according to the conditions: "It was right after the war in Japan when living conditions were the worst and the people had lost any peace they may have had in their mind. A poor old blind

lady called Nobu, who lived in a corner of a burnt
and devastated area, came to worship at a temple,
and quite joyously said to the priest of the temple:
'Reverend, I have had a light placed near my
house.' 'Did you! Why?' asked the priest. [Nobu
replied], 'It is outside my room. My room is in a
tenement house in the midst of an alley. The walk
is in a terrible condition, and at night it is very
dangerous for people to pass through. I have long
wanted to place a light for them.'"[14]

In this book, I have used a number of metaphors
to express the varieties of spiritual transformation—
born again, *open heart*, *conversion*, and *calling*.
In chapter 2, I wrote about crossing the waters.
The idea of *crossing* is a metaphor for the process
of spiritual transformation—leaving daily life and
going to a special place, a thin place, in which one
is in contact with sacred processes, with events of
grace, that continually transform the universe and
peoples' lives. *Crossing* also is a metaphor for the
return, from transformative places and times, back
to daily life. As we remember and reflect on such
crossings in our own lives, we might think about
how our identities change, how we may become
transformed from closed to open hearts, how we
may experience callings to serve others, and how
in the midst of calamities and death, we, like Nobu,
can become persons who live now in eternity with
bliss-bestowing hands.

Notes

Preface

1. William James, *Essays in Radical Empiricism* (New York: Longmans, Green and Co., 1938).

2. Nancy Frankenberry, "Major Themes of Empirical Theology," in *Empirical Theology: A Handbook*, ed. Randolph Crump Miller (Birmingham, Ala.: Religious Education, 1992), 45.

3. Star Island is an island with conference and lodging facilities, which is maintained by Star Island Corporation, a nonprofit organization. According to Brad Greeley, president of Star Island Corporation, Star Island aspires be "a place for renewal, personal growth, connection." For more of Brad Greeley's letter to potential visitors of Star Island and for more information on Star Island, you may wish to visit www.starisland.org. For more information on IRAS, please see www.iras.org.

1. On the Edge of Time

1. Nikos Kazantzakis, *Report to Greco* (New York: Simon and Shuster, 1965), 291–92, quoted in John B. Cobb Jr., *God and the World* (Philadelphia: Westminster, 1976), 53. Passage modified by Karl E. Peters to use inclusive language.

2. Terrence W. Deacon, *The Symbolic Species: The Co-Evolution of Language and the Brain* (New York: W. W. Norton, 1997).

3. Gordon Kaufman, *Jesus and Creativity* (Minneapolis: Fortress Press, 2007), 63–88.

4. Here I am following the thinking of medical ethicist William F. May, *The Patient's Ordeal* (Bloomington: Indiana University Press, 1991), 9–12. I'll return to May's formulation more specifically in chapter 8, "Calamitous Convergences."

5. Paul Tillich, *Systematic Theology*, vol. 1 (Chicago: University of Chicago Press, 1951), 11–15.

6. Henry Nelson Wieman, *Man's Ultimate Commitment* (Carbondale: Southern Illinois University Press, 1958), 91–92, 290–97.

7. May, *The Patient's Ordeal*, 12.

8. *The Spiritual Transformation Scientific Research Program* (Philadelphia: The Metanexus Institute on Religion and Science, 2004), 5. See http://www.metanexus.net/spiritual_transformation/news/STRP%20Prospectus%202004_high.pdf (accessed April 4, 2008).

9. Ibid., 8.

10. Acts 17:28.

11. Augustine, Book 7, in *Confessions*, trans. R. S. Pine-Coffin (New York: Penguin Books, 1961).

12. Henry Nelson Wieman, *The Source of Human Good* (Carbondale: Southern Illinois University Press, 1946), 54–58.

2. Crossings

1. Heinrich Zimmer, *Philosophies of India*, ed. Joseph Campbell (Princeton: Princeton University Press, 1989), 477–79. Modified to be gender inclusive by Karl E. Peters.

2. Papers from that conference can be found in *Zygon: Journal of Religion and Science,* 1986 (March and June).

3. John Y. Fenton and others, *Religions of Asia*, 3rd ed. (New York: St. Martin's, 1993), 4–16.

4. Ibid., 7–9.

5. Louis Finkelstein, "Nothing Is Ordinary," in *The Ways of Religion*, 3rd ed., ed. Roger Eastman (New York: Oxford University Press, 1999), 294. From *The Jews* by Louis Finkelstein (New York: HarperCollins, 1960). I have changed the passage to include inclusive language.

6. Ibid., 294.

7. Catherine L. Albanese, *America: Religions and Religion*, 2d ed. (Belmont, Calif.: Wadsworth, 1992), 6–9.

8. Marjorie Davis, personal communication. She told me about this incident after she and I were married in 1999. Marj became my second wife after my first wife of over thirty years, Carol, died in 1995.

9. Eugene G. d'Aquili, "The Neurobiological Bases of Myth and Concepts of Deity," *Zygon: Journal of Religion and Science* 13 (December 1978): 257–74.

3. Passages

1. Lewis Joseph Sherrill, *The Struggle of the Soul: A Picture of the Crucial Stages of Human Spiritual Development from Childhood to Old Age* (New York: Macmillan, 1963), 25, 39. The language has been modified by Karl E. Peters to make it inclusive.

2. Philip Hefner, "Spiritual Transformation—An Encounter with the Sacred" (lecture, 52nd Annual Conference of the Institute on Religion in an Age of Science, Star Island, N.H., July 31, 2005).

3. Internal Family Systems Conference 2005, University of Saint Mary's of the Lake, Mundelein, Ill., September 16–18, 2005.

4. Rebirths

1. Marcus J. Borg, *The Heart of Christianity* (San Francisco: HarperSanFrancisco, 2003), 117–9.

2. Aldo Leopold, *A Sand County Almanac, With Essays on Conservation from Round River* (New York: Balantine Books, 1970), 240.

3. Borg, *Heart of Christianity*, 149.

4. Ibid., 151-54, 161-63.

5. Ibid., 162.

6. Ibid., 162.

7. Ibid., 163.

8. Lewis Joseph Sherrill, *The Struggle of the Soul: A Picture of the Crucial Stages of Human Spiritual Development from Childhood to Old Age* (New York: Macmillan, 1963), 39.

9. Pierre Teilhard de Chardin, *The Divine Milieu* (New York: Harper, 1960).

10. Borg, *Heart of Christianity*, 156.

11. Ursula Goodenough, *Sacred Depths of Nature* (New York: Oxford University Press, 1998).

5. Conversion

1. William James, *The Varieties of Religious Experience* (New York: Simon & Schuster, 1997), 160.

2. John Hick, *God Has Many Names* (Philadelphia: Westminster, 1982), 9.

3. See Richard C. Schwartz, *Internal Family Systems Therapy* (New York: Guilford Press, 1995), especially the chapter, "Viewing Individuals as Systems," 27–60. My presentation here follows that of Marjorie H. Davis, "One Thing Needful," a sermon at the First Congregational Church of Granby, Conn., February 27, 2000.

4. James, *Varieties*, 163.

5. Schwartz, *Internal Family Systems*, 46-52.

6. See Melvin Konner, the chapters on "Fear" and its roots, and on "Love" including parent-child bonding, in *The Tangled Wing: Biological Constraints on the Human Spirit* (New York: Henry Holt, 2002), 204–35, 297–336.

7. Konner, "Rage," *Tangled Wing*, 182-87.

8. James, *Varieties*, 160.

9. Lewis Rambo, *Understanding Religious Conversion* (New Haven: Yale University Press, 1993), esp. 7–12.

10. Thich Nhat Hanh, *Living Buddha, Living Christ* (New York: Penguin Putnam, Riverhead Books, 1997), 16, 17.

11. Eugene d'Aquili and Andrew B. Newberg, *The Mystical Mind: Probing the Biology of Religious Experience* (Minneapolis: Fortress Press, 1999), 109–10.

12. Huston Smith, interviewed by Bill Moyers, "Hinduism and Buddhism," *The Wisdom of Faith with Huston Smith*, the Moyers Collection on DVD (Princeton: Films for the Humanities and the Sciences, 2004).

13. Thich Nhat Hanh, *Living Buddha*, 14.

14. Ibid., 20.

6. Callings

1. Karl E. Peters, *Dancing with the Sacred* (Harrisburg, Pa.: Trinity International, 2002), 36.

2. James Watson, *The Double Helix: A Personal Account of the Discovery of the Structure of DNA* (New York: Penguin Putnam, 1991).

3. Gordon D. Kaufman, *Theology for a Nuclear Age* (Philadelphia: Westminster, 1985), 40.

4. Ibid., 40–41.

5. For example, John Dewey: *Logic, The Theory of Inquiry* (New York: H. Holt and Company, 1938).

6. One can note here a parallel with Victor Turner's model of spiritual transformation that I've been using. See chapters 2 and 5.

7. For example, Peters, *Dancing*, 47, 52–59.

8. Arthur Peacocke "A Naturalistic Christian Faith for the Twenty-First Century: An Essay in Interpretation," in *All That Is: A Naturalistic Christian Faith for the Twenty-First Century*, ed. Philip Clayton (Minneapolis: Fortress Press, 2007), 26–29. See also my essay "Empirical Theology and a 'Naturalistic Christian Faith,'" in ibid., 99–103.

9. See http://www.cassadaga.org. For an introduction to American Spiritualism, see Catherine L. Albanese, *America: Religions and Religion*, 2d ed. (Belmont, Calif.: Wadsworth, 1992), 262–66.

10. At the 52nd Annual Conference of the Institute on Religion in an Age of Science, later on the same morning that I gave the chapel talk that is the basis for this chapter, Joan Koss-Chioino talked about such spiritual realities, "Radical Empathy: The Divide between Ritual Healing and Medical Therapies" (lecture, 52nd Annual Conference of the Institute on Religion in an Age of Science, Star Island, N.H., August 2, 2005).

7. Events of Grace

1. Denise L. Carmody and John T. Carmody, *Christianity: An Introduction* (Belmont, Calif.: Wadsworth, 1983), 20.

2. Henry Nelson Wieman, *The Source of Human Good* (Carbondale, Ill.: Southern Illinois University Press,1946), 133.

3. Carmody and Carmody, *Christianity*, 20.

4. This was a meeting of the Ecumenical Roundtable on Science, Technology and the Church, an annual gathering

of science and religious groups from various Christian denominations.

5. Isaiah 2:4.

8. Calamitous Convergences

1. Joan D. Chittister, *Scarred by Struggle, Transformed by Hope* (Grand Rapids, Mich.: William B. Eerdmans, 2003), 84–85.

2. See Arthur Peacocke's chapter, "A Naturalistic Christian Faith for the Twenty-First Century: An Essay in Interpretation," and Karl E. Peter's chapter "Empirical Theology and a 'Naturalistic Christian Faith,'" in *All That Is: A Naturalistic Christian Faith for the Twenty-First Century*, ed. Philip Clayton (Minneapolis: Fortress Press, 2007).

3. See, Karl E. Peters, *Dancing with the Sacred* (Harrisburg: Trinity International, 2002), 36.

4. Nicholas Evans, *The Horse Whisperer* (New York: Dell, 1996), 1–20.

5. William F. May, *The Patient's Ordeal* (Bloomington: Indiana University Press, 1991), 9–12.

6. Ibid., 11.

7. Ibid., 12.

8. Ursula Goodenough and Paul Woodruff, "Mindful Virtue, Mindful Reverence," *Zygon: Journal of Religion and Science* 36 (December 2001): 585–95.

9. Ibid., 590, 592.

10. Ibid., 586.

11. Jean Kristeller, "Varieties of Spiritual Experience and Health Effects" (lecture, 52nd Annual Conference of the Institute on Religion in an Age of Science, Star Island, N.H., August 2, 2005).

12. What I'm describing here is developed more fully in my essay, "Spiritual Transformation and Healing in Light of an Evolutionary Theology," in *Spiritual Transformation and Healing*, ed. Joan D. Koss-Chioino and Philip Hefner (Lanham, Md.: AltaMira, 2006).

13. Daniela Altimari, "A Little Girl, a Lofty Legacy," *The Hartford Courant*, August 3, 2004, http://pqasb.pqarchiver.com/courant/access/ (accessed February 20, 2008).

9. Dying

1. Robert T. Weston, "Out of the Stars," *Singing the Living Tradition* (Boston: Beacon Press, the Unitarian Universalist Association, 1993), no. 530. Used by permission.

2. Bruce Greyson, "Near-Death Experiences and Spirituality," *Zygon: Journal of Religion and Science* 41 (June 2006): 394.

3. Ibid., 393.

4. My most profound experience of this was during the dying of my first wife Carol over a period of fifteen months. See Karl E. Peters, "From Life to Love," in *Dancing with the Sacred* (Harrisburg: Trinity International, 2002), 117–18.

10. Living Now in Eternity

1. Max Rudolf Lemberg, "The Complementarity of Religion and Science: A Trialogue," *Zygon: Journal of Religion and Science* 14 (December 1979): 373–74. Passage modified by Karl E. Peters to use inclusive language.

2. Augustine, Book 11, in *Confessions*, trans. R. S. Pine-Coffin (New York: Penguin Books, 1961).

3. Louis Finkelstein, "Nothing Is Ordinary," in *The Ways of Religion*, 3d ed., ed. Roger Eastman (New York: Oxford University Press, 1999).

4. Lemberg, "The Complementarity of Religion and Science," 373.

5. Sir Julian Huxley, Introduction to *The Phenomenon of Man*, by Pierre Teilhard de Chardin (New York: Harper & Row, 1965), 20.

6. Some examples of this story being told are Brian Swimme and Thomas Berry, *The Universe Story* (San Francisco: HarperSanFrancisco, 1992); Loyal Rue, *Everybody's Story: Wising Up to the Epic of Evolution* (Albany: State University of New York Press, 2000); and all the essays and resources on Connie Barlow and Michael Dowd's Web site, "The Great Story," at http://www.thegreatstory.org (accessed April 4, 2008).

7. Aldo Leopold, *A Sand County Almanac: With Essays on Conservation from Round River* (New York: Ballantine Books, 1970), 240.

8. Huston Smith, "Tao Now: An Ecological Testament," in *Earth Might Be Fair: Reflections on Ethics, Religion, and Ecology*, ed. Ian Barbour (Englewood Cliffs, N.J.: Prentice-Hall, 1972), 62–81.

9. Heinrich Schütz, *The Christmas Story*, ed. Arthur Mendel (New York: G. Schirmer, 1949).

10. Zenkei Shibayama, *A Flower Does Not Talk* (North Clarendon, Vt.: Tuttle Publishing, 1970).

11. See "The Ten Oxherding Pictures of Zen: Series 2," on the Zen Buddhist Order of Hsu Yun Web site, http://www.hsuyun.org/Dharma/zbohy/VisualArts/OxHerding Pictures/oxherding2.html.

12. Ibid., 200–201.

13. Ibid., 203.

14. Ibid., 203.